MW01156492

Experts Praise *Gifts From The Child Within*

"*Gifts From The Child Within* is more than a well-written, well-researched guide to recovery from our childhood wounds. It is an exciting adventure in psychospiritual growth based on inner wisdom exercises that are a powerful addition to the archives of healing."

Joan Borysenko, Ph.D., Author
Your Soul's Compass

"*Gifts From The Child Within* is a skillfully written book about a significant subject. Dr. Sinor describes a broad range of valuable tools for healing the child within each of us. Her extensive research has yielded an excellent choice of quotes from many important sources. A fine storyteller, she further anchors her message with fascinating stories and examples ranging from Grimm to her own Hypnotherapy practice. Most importantly, the book details many powerful processes that the reader can use for substantial benefits with self-hypnosis."

Randal Churchill, CHT,
Director Hypnotherapy Training Institute
President, American Council of Hypnotist Examiners

"*Gifts From The Child Within* offers many techniques for therapists working with Adult Children of Alcoholics and is a therapeutic aid to re-discovery of self and subsequent change. This book is a useful tool for any therapist and a wonderful adjunct to one's therapy. Dr. Sinor has found a means within her book to award a 'guide' to the past and a 'strength' to continue into the future."

Nancy New, Ph.D.

"Barbara Sinor has written a book that will help the violated and traumatized child within to heal. Recovery is a barbaric journey. *Gifts From The Child Within* helps guide survivors with repressed memories of trauma, as well as those with current memories of incest, through the healing process."

Marilyn Van Derbur, *Miss America* 1958
Founder, Survivors United Network

"[we wish you] ...the best of success with *Gifts From The Child Within*, we look forward to its impact within the recovery field. We are grateful for your contribution."

Gerald S. Myers, President & CEO
Suzanne Somers Institute

"Dr. Sinor has bridged the gap for clients and therapists alike between the mere discovery of the inner child and the building of a true relationship with this most important being within. *Gifts From The Child Within* is an important and highly readable work."

Rick Boyes, M.A., CHT, *A Body To Die For*

"Part of what makes recovery books useful for so many people is the array of diverse approaches offered in the self-help genre. In *Gifts From The Child Within*, Dr. Sinor shares her own story and unique vantage point in exercises and affirmations that seek to rework, rewrite, and *re-create* past, hurtful experiences that may interfere with present-day living."

Nancy J. Napier, M.A., MFCC, Author
Recreating Your Self

"*Gifts From The Child Within* is a wonderful book that takes the reader on a journey into the soul via the 'time-traveling machine of the subconscious mind.' Dr. Barbara Sinor writes with sensitivity and clarity revealing her deep knowledge of hypnotherapy and transpersonal psychology. She invites you to become a participant by exploring your own childhood and reveals intimate and fascinating details from her own. Flowing and readable, this book is filled with stories, myths, information and revelation."

Marilyn Gordon, CHT, Author
Healing is Remembering Who You Are

"[I am]...impressed with the focus and exercises found in *Gifts From The Child Within*. Father Leo Booth advocates the 'whole person' approach to therapy and healing, and always advises doing inner child exercises as integral steps to healing wounded spirituality.... this book is a valuable resource; it is definitely one we will add to our own reference library."

Katharine Russell, Editorial Director *Spiritual Concepts*

"*Gifts From The Child Within* contributes to the much needed "wave of healing" currently happening in society. Dr. Sinor shows a sensitive understanding of how childhood distress and trauma affect us as adults; and she gives effective techniques for accessing the inner child part of us and for releasing blockages and emotions. These methods truly apply well to the recovery process and I am applying them effectively with ACAs and with others carrying emotional and behavioral scars from childhood. Thank you, Barbara, for your practical messages of hope for healing ourselves and for becoming more creative, happy adults!"

Barbara Lamb, M.S., MFCC

"*Gifts From The Child Within* is a sensitively written book totally free of the strain of self-pity found in many of the "wounded child" books. Dr. Barbara Sinor has given us an important self-help program based on her own healing experience, while keeping her work clinically sound and very well documented. The book is based on the premise that if we can accept, at least in part, responsibility the illusional reality of our past conditioning, we are then ready to re-create it into a reality for our present.

By following these guidelines perhaps we can stop the generational cycle of patterning that seems to have followed us from the beginning of time. Dr. Sinor has given us another, significant message overlooked by other writers, teachers and therapists. Not only does she show us how to get in touch with and love our child within, she helps us look further to recognize the gifts the child has to give in return. I highly recommend this book for the hypnotherapist, the counselor, the teacher and as a self-help course for people anywhere who are seeking the road to recovery."

Lavona Stillman, Ph.D., CCHT
Stillman Institute for Research & Development

Gifts From The Child Within

Second Edition

A workbook for self-discovery and self-recovery through Re-Creation Therapy™

Barabara Sinor, PhD

Library of Congress Cataloging-in-Publication Data

Sinor, Barbara, 1945-
    Gifts from the child within : self-discovery and self-recovery
through re-creation therapy(tm) / Barabara Sinor. -- 2nd ed.
        p. cm.
    Includes bibliographical references and index.
    ISBN-13: 978-1-932690-46-0 (trade paper : alk. paper)
    ISBN-10: 1-932690-46-8 (trade paper : alk. paper)
    1. Inner child. 2. Self-help techniques. 3. Psychotherapy--
Popular works. I. Title.
    BF698.35.I55S56 2008
    616.89'14--dc22

                                        2007047234

Acknowledgement is made for permission to reprint the following:
From *Emmanuel's Book II* by Pat Rodegast and Judith Stanton,
Copyright 1989 by Pat Rodegast and Judith Stanton. Used by permis-
sion of Bantam Books, a division of Bantam Doubleday Dell Publish-
ing Group, Inc.
"The Stubborn Child" and "The Three Lazy Sons" from *The Com-
plete Fairy Tales of the Brothers Grimm* by Jack Zipes, translator,
translation copyright 1987 by Jack Zipes. Used by permission of
Bantam Books, a division of Bantam Doubleday Dell Publishing
Group, Inc.
Cover art: *The Child Within* by Paula B. Slater, M.A. All rights re-
served.

Distributed by: Baker & Taylor, Ingram Book Group
Published by:
Loving Healing Press
5145 Pontiac Trail
Ann Arbor, MI 48105

http://www.LovingHealing.com or
info@LovingHealing.com
Fax +1 734 663 6861

Loving Healing Press

Table of Contents

Dedication

I dedicate this book to Richard and Cindy Sinor. In many ways you both have taught me that a family can continue to develop its support and intimacy for one another even when seemingly apart. As each of you read this book you may identify with your own child within. Bright-eyed Richie who was always ready to help with his younger sister and talkative little Cindy who never wanted to go to bed will always be with you. The unique inner child that you each possess will also forever be a part of *my* life. I have watched in expectation those two small children mature into talented young adults. This dedication is my way of saying "thank you" for allowing me to participate in the joys and sorrows of your past and present.

Remember what your Grandpa used to say? "Your family is the most important thing in life."

He was right.

Barbara Sinor, Ph.D.
January 2008

Foreword

"Take her in my arms and love her? Why? I don't even like her!" my client sounded astonished and resentful. She wanted no part of the inner child and was aggravated by the implication that she was somehow responsible for her own dilemma. This client had been with me for three hypnotherapeutic sessions. The process of childhood age regression effectively re-created the feelings: A feeling of abandonment when her father died; feeling alone in the loveless relationship she had had with her father; and feeling the abusive entanglements of her mother's alcoholism. I had done a hypnotherapeutic interweave after each session. She seemed to be working positively through each stab of abuse and each scar of memory. But she simply would not accept that the inner child—her Beingness—had constantly given away her personal power in an endless, repetitive "trying to please everyone" type of behavior.

This client and I found the way out of the abyss of her denial and unfolded a vital spirit capable of successful interpersonal relationships. If *Gifts From The Child Within* had been available, I would have given her homework. From the first session she would have benefited from reading the exercises, the "Child Within Autohypnosis" visualizations, and the material in the chapter "Facing and For-giving Yourself." I believe the reading of these sections would have helped facilitate her effective outcome from her hypnotherapy sessions.

To me there is a very important ingredient in *Gifts From The Child Within*. This ingredient is the knowledge that each individual must proceed through his/her life discoveries, or in therapeutic intervention at one's own rate, with one's own sense of how things are and with one's own resolutions. The therapist is ill-advised to mold and shape the individual toward a patterned behavior or personality cubby-hole—one which is controlled by the therapist based upon concepts rather than upon individualized actual experience emotionally constructed and attitudinally integrated by the individual through the life moments of choice and action.

Some years ago a client came to me after seeking help through every available avenue. Our therapeutic relationship flourished. He commented that he stayed with me and was able to withstand recovery because as he put it, "she keeps her cotton-picking hands off my psyche!" His inner child was so deeply buried he felt like his "entire being was in a tantrum." By allowing him to go at his own pace and pretty much facilitate his own sessions, his child within cautiously emerged. After each session he functioned more capably in the world. Today he is free to love his child within and live fully.

Dr. Milton Erickson consistently had great success with clients from all walks of life, all ages, and with every conceivable kind of problem because he was able to enter the client's world and hear as the client heard. He did not impose nor force-feed his own view of how the world is or how the client should behave. Unfortunately many therapists impose their views and determinations upon their clients resulting in short-term help and eventual relapse. Dr. Erickson admonished therapists not to plan therapy but to allow the events of each session to guide the client's subconscious mind to direct the therapy. Re-Creation Therapy™ accomplishes this task.

Dr. Sinor has a very pragmatic, yet creative application of the general ideas of Alice Miller. In her this book, she utilizes re-creation exercises which are useful for professional application and for persons learning a new way of being. I have seen Barbara's concepts at work in my practicum sessions for advanced hypnotherapy training. One previous student of mine demonstrated a re-creation exercise that she had learned while attending one of Dr. Sinor's seminars. I was amazed and delighted at the effective use of Re-Creation Therapy™ and thankful that Barbara had created a readable, useful, and authoritative resource for us all.

As you read this book, you will find that Dr. Sinor presents a paradigm for empowering yourself or a client to solve problems working with body, mind, emotions, and spirit. We are all healing together on Universal levels. In this regard, Alice Miller believed that all of us are victims of "child rear-

ing" and that most of the abuse to children is well inten-
tioned. Parents raised their children the way their parents
raised them. In the added Afterword to the Second Edition
(1984) of *For Your Own Good*, Miller lists twelve points to
amplify her meaning. These points include:

> 1. All children, for their development, need to be
> respected and taken seriously so that they can ex-
> press their love, be loved in return, grow up with un-
> damaged integrity, and with the ability to be
> responsive, intelligent, loving and highly sensitive.
> 2. When children are abused, exploited and not
> allowed to express their anger and pain, they sup-
> press these feelings to the point that they have no
> memory of them.
> 3. As adults and parents, they then often take
> revenge on their own children and/or society because
> their childhood repression, though unremembered,
> exerts a powerful influence over them.
> 4. It is society in general and children in particu-
> lar who suffer and pay the price for this. Yes society
> still sanctions abusive child rearing methods.

Gifts From The Child Within acknowledges these facts and
Dr. Sinor quite honestly shares with us the pain of her own
childhood; then like the golden dawn coming to a dark bleak
morning, she also shares her own journey toward wholeness
and presents a process for self-healing. It is a sensitively
written book totally free of the strain of self-pity found in
many of the "wounded child" books. By following the guidelines within this book, perhaps we can stop the generational
cycle of patterning that seems to have followed us from the
beginning of time.

Dr. Barbara Sinor has shown us how to get in touch with
and love our child within; release negative emotions; re-
create childhood beliefs and experiences; and to look further,
in recognition of all the gifts the child within has for us who
have the courage and wisdom to look within. This is indeed a
valuable self-help book, a tool for the Counselor, Hypnotherapist, Minister, Psychotherapist, or Clinician. Dr. Sinor

has given all mental health professionals an invaluable paradigm for use in Inner Child work. I assure you, the world will
look much brighter after you read this book.

Lavona Stillman, Ph.D., CC.HT.
Stillman Institute for Research & Development
Santa Clara, California
First Edition, August 1993

Introduction

> "Re-Creation Therapy™ is a transforming process of reaching, touching, and accepting the child within us; the process continues with a releasing of blockages and emotions, and finally, the re-creating of past emotional trauma to re-form the creative vital force found within the adult."

The above definition of Re-Creation Therapy™ was written many years ago. I have worked with this enriching and rewarding process for over twenty-five years and have found a great personal sense of healing and recovery from the wounds of my childhood. In the late 1970s, while trying desperately to make sense of my negative childhood experiences, recent divorce, plummeting career, and general lack of motivation, I chose to study counseling.

Soon I realized that most of the women who came to the clinic where I was working were locked into their childhood conditioning and experiences. I began investigating my own inner beliefs and self-concepts and discovered that I, too, saw myself and my world through the eyes of my little girl buried deep inside me. I recognized this child within was still trying desperately to get the attention and approval she so desired from her parents.

During the early 1980s, I developed the basic principles of Re-Creation Therapy™ through many hours of self-exploration and testing. The techniques and exercises in this book have evolved during my initial counseling practice and my own recovery years of being a child of an alcoholic father who demonstrated inappropriate behavior with my sisters and myself, as well as, a codependent mother. I have had the opportunity to introduce the healing techniques of Re-Creation Therapy™ to many clients who have re-created their own negative childhood conditioning and trauma into new personal successes of recovery.

Re-Creation Therapy™ is based on, and is an expansion of, the concept of the child within each of us. Working with the various methods and tools found within this book, your inner child becomes a messenger who brings long awaited information regarding the origin of your present beliefs, values, and motivations. Many of the suggested exercises and methods are derived from my Transpersonal Counseling background. As you discover and explore your child within memories and move through past experiences and emotions, you will appreciate how these transpersonal methods allow you to move with your own rhythms and direction. This type of guiding therapy encourages one to seek inner wisdom rather than a pre-set therapeutic directive. You will become aware of hidden childhood beliefs and emotions and begin to realize and use your adult "power of choice" and to learn how to *re-create your own reality.*

The past is but a memory locked within the subconscious mind. Recent research into the areas of human consciousness is bringing us evidence that "memory must be non-physical, metaphysical or spiritual in nature." In reading and experiencing this book, you will learn there are no time barriers to reaching your vast storehouse of memories. You can create a positive present by re-creating the past with the use of Hypnotherapy (or autohypnosis), Creative Visualization, and other Transpersonal Counseling techniques.

I choose to study and work with Hypnotherapy for it fills my spiritual needs in searching for my inner-most Self. Hypnotherapy is a rewarding and enlightening tool for self-discovery and self-recovery. If you have reservations regarding the use of hypnosis, let me assure you that hypnosis is a very *safe* journey inward to explore your own subconscious mind. You are *totally* in control.

Some of the most common misconceptions about the use of hypnosis are:
- I will pass out
- I won't be in control of myself
- My mind will be weakened
- I might tell the therapist secrets
- I may not awaken from the "trance"
- I will behave in an unacceptable manner

ALL OF THE ABOVE STATEMENTS ARE FALSE

Hypnosis and Hypnotherapy can:

- Induce relaxation
- Help control (or alleviate) pain
- Overcome habitual addictions
- Instill a sense of calm and peace
- Arouse latent creativity
- Release fears and phobias
- Reduce stress, both emotional and physical
- Create positive growth patterns
- Effect behavioral changes, and
- Employ age regression as an emotional release and healing tool

Add to the above list a most important outcome derived from hypnotherapy: *The realization that you have control over and can manifest your own reality.* That we "create our own reality" is becoming more and more evident to the expanded minds of today. We realize what we are at present is the outcome of what we have thought, acted upon, reacted to, and believed ourselves to be. We are today literally the sum total of our experiences, perceptions, and beliefs. With this belief, we become a co-creator of our reality and can choose to re-create our experiences, perceptions, and beliefs thereby shaping a reality by choice, not mere acceptance of what we believed we must accept. One of this therapy's highest rewards is this "consciousness of Self" in relation to God/ Goddess/All That Is.

In Part I of the book, I explain in detail the concept of the Child Within and urge the reader to explore and reach for this small voice inside. Along with various exercises to help this connection unfold, the basic foundations of Re-Creation Therapy™ are presented. Part II and III delve into many of the core issues surrounding the blockages many of us as adults today have had to face because of our childhood experiences, as well as, offering many exercises, autohypnosis visualizations, affirmations, and other techniques to begin the journey of recovery.

I suggest you start at your own pace as you forge ahead on this healing journey taking the time to explore and *feel* the emotions which surface along the way. The last few Chapters address the avenues we can take to ensure our awareness of this healing jaunt and offer insight for the future. Remembering that our actions, thoughts, beliefs and values are all based upon our awareness of our reality, we can accept our reality as (at least partially) of our own making. With this knowledge, we can proceed to heal it—for in the final analysis, we all heal ourselves.

We are constantly testing ourselves and our reality. There is no finish line. There is no ribbon signifying an end to the race for recovery. It is an ongoing race. Our competition?

Ourselves.

Barbara Sinor, Ph.D.
Second Edition 2008

**The names and sequences of experiences related in this book have been altered to protect the anonymity of the people who have shared their stories.

Part I

The
Child Within

"Somewhere, sometime, you were a child."
—W. Hugh Missildine

1 The Concept of the Child Within

"...the child symbolizes the pre-conscious and the post-conscious essence of man."
—C.G. Jung

When I was a little girl, my family lived near a reservoir called Puddingstone Dam. It was used for recreational fishing, boating, and swimming by the local communities. On hot summer days my Mother, two sisters, and I would wait for Daddy to come home from work then head off for our favorite swimming spot. The water deepened gradually where we swam, so I was able to "fake it" for many years. You see, I was almost nine years old before learning to really swim.

I will never forget how much I wanted to please my Father by swimming across the roped-off area. Even my younger sister was swimming and diving off the raft out in the deep end by three years old! I desperately wanted to receive the praise and smiles she was commanding from Daddy. I was so afraid to bring *both* my feet up to kick that for many years I would keep one foot on the bottom while kicking on the surface with the other foot making it *look* like I was swimming. Then one summer Daddy decided to test me. He literally picked me up and threw me into the deep water. I immediately learned to swim with both feet kicking high!

What I remember most about this swimming episode was not the trauma of how I learned to swim but my "feelings" surrounding the need for Daddy's approval. As a child, I would have done anything he asked to get his approval—and I did. He was a big-hearted, self-engrossed alcoholic and I bought right into the typical codependent, self-effacing, self-sacrificing role of the child adult, later becoming an adult child.

Through my adult years, I studied, researched, analyzed, have been analyzed, and worked with my personal childhood trauma resulting from living in a dysfunctional family. I learned a great deal about my child within and the different concepts for healing and recovery. During the 1980s to present, I have been fortunate to experience and clinically introduce a healing process which directly addresses the phenomenon of healing the wounded inner child. Whether seeking recovery from drug or alcohol abuse, codependency, victimization, physical, emotional or spiritual abuse, or the trauma of living in a dysfunctional family, Re-Creation Therapy™ may be the long awaited guidance for which you have been searching.

Can you remember your childhood? Can you consciously recall a particular age and sense your emotions at that time in your life? If you were asked to close your eyes and visualize yourself at the age of five or twelve, could you sense or see yourself at this age? Can you imagine the surroundings where you grew up and/or the emotions you felt? Can you remember the qualities you liked or disliked about your mother, father, relatives, teachers, or friends during your childhood years? There may be several different memories within each year of your childhood. All these, as well as, the ones you do not recall are held tight within your subconscious mind by your child within.

As we become adults, we learn to put aside our childhood, believing it to be over and that the past no longer matters. However, the child within us still plays, laughs, cries, yells, desires attention and needs love. Our inner child is usually adventuresome, curious, fearful and nervous, inventive, caring and compassionate; but most importantly, it is a part of us. The experiential exercises, visualizations, and techniques within this book will help you rediscover your child within, which in turn will lead you to forgotten memories, unfulfilled dreams, past woundedness, and outmoded beliefs which may be blocking a more creative, successful adult life.

Conceptual Background

The concept of the inner child is not a new one. When renowned psychotherapist Carl G. Jung talked of the "inner child archetype," he was referring to the universal unconscious mindset found within the "Collective Unconscious."

However, Jung also noted an individual inner child, a child which actually exists within each adult. Jung explained, "The child motif is a picture of certain *forgotten* things in our childhood.... [it] represents the preconscious, childhood aspect of the collective psyche."

One noted psychoanalyst of the 1950s, Eric Berne, spoke of the aspect of the "child" as one of the ego components in his Transactional Analysis (TA) process. The other two ego components of TA are the "parent" and the "adult." Berne's TA theory of human personality demonstrates how each ego state directs our individual lives. Berne's intent was to find "the briefest, most economical way for his clients to increase their autonomy by reawakening their potential for awareness, spontaneity, and intimacy—capacities which are inherent in all of us, but which are sometimes limited as a result of the stresses and traumas of growing up."

Many feel Berne's personality theory to be a close glimpse of the child within concept but disagree with Berne's labeling the inner child an "ego state." Perhaps the word *ego* is too strong when describing these three personality components and the term "aspect" might be more suitable to denote the fine line divisions between the adult, parent, and child selves. These three aspects are parts of our personality and are linked to an "inner core"—the higher spiritual-self—which is most readily connected to the child within.

Charles Whitfield, doctor and author, introduces the "healing nature" of the child within through the recovery process found in the widely emerging Adult Children of Alcoholics (ACoA) groups. In his book, *Healing the Child Within: Discovery and Recovery for Adult Children of Dysfunctional Families*, Whitfield states,

> "When the Child Within is not nurtured or allowed freedom of expression, a false or codependent self emerges. We begin to live our lives from a victim stance, and experience difficulties in resolving emotional traumas. The gradual accumulation of unfinished mental and emotional business can lead to chronic anxiety, fear, confusion, emptiness and unhappiness."

We can recapture our emotional stability and independence-of-self by allowing ourselves to remember, experience, and communicate with this hidden child within who learned so aptly to adapt to his or her environment as a means of tactical survival. During a workshop I attended (May 1990) Whitfield commented that most alcoholics start out being a "child adult" learning to cope with many adult responsibilities as a child, then later, they become an "adult child."

There are many therapists who have given us insight into the concept of the child within, one such master of hypnosis is Milton Erickson. Erickson was one of the earliest founders of the child within concept via his renown work with Hypnotherapy. His research and clinical work with literally thousands of patients has revealed truly miraculous techniques and methods for healing and recovery.

One of Erickson's more noted case histories exploring the child within is that of "The February Man" in which he draws on psychotherapeutic age regression techniques. One of his methods surrounding this important work is the hypnotic tool of "reframing" (developing new frames of reference for the past). Erickson demonstrates just how inseparable the mind/body phenomenon is in this case of a client who has a fear of being able to adequately raise her child-to-be because of her lack of secure familial ties in childhood.

During therapy, Erickson introduced to his client's "subconscious mind" a friend, a confidant. This fatherly figure was brought into the age regression sessions while she was in a hypnotic state. Over a succession of meetings, Erickson repeatedly employed techniques of age regression incorporated with an amnesia effect so his client would not recall this fictitious acquaintance in a conscious waking state of mind. The use of age regression facilitated Erickson's success in generating past real-life memories which were intertwined with the use of indirect hypnotic suggestions regarding the fictional "February Man" (later named because he had met this client in the month of February).

Erickson demonstrated perfectly with this case that there is no separation of mind/body—for change in belief structure precedes the body's experience. In other words, *belief pre-*

cedes experience and change. When Erickson's client firmly embraced on a subconscious level that she had been aided and cared for by the February Man in her childhood, she was able to re-create her fear and apprehension into stability and confidence in her ability to raise her unborn child.

Re-Creation Therapy™ employs a form of Hypnotherapy which incorporates the main theme of age regression and reframing employed by Erickson. This process can be executed alone by using self-hypnosis (autohypnosis) or with the assistance of a Hypnotherapist. This emotional release therapy introduces tools to acknowledge, meet, and communicate with one's inner child. A new frame of reference is established which brings with it a clear, enlightened view of *who you are becoming.*

You can release limiting emotions, fears, and inappropriate patterns which bind you to your parents and the learned *behavior* of the past. While in the state of guided hypnosis, or within autohypnosis, a new element of reference can be introduced to the subconscious mind. An unpleasant event can be re-created into a positive experience; or you can re-create a totally different scenario altogether to wash away old fears, rejections, or childhood turmoil. As with Erickson's reframing methods which made it "...possible to introduce a new element not actually belonging to the situation but that could easily fit into it," the process of Re-Creation Therapy™ allows you to touch the hidden past of your child within and *re-create your own reality* making it suitable to you now as an adult.

Illusional Reality

We all use adaptability in one form or another in childhood to "fit-in" and gain approval. However, like my trick of deceiving my family that I really knew how to swim, many of the traits, beliefs, and feelings we adopt may not be sufficient for a healthy adulthood. Do you rely on childhood behaviors of adaptability to help you gain acceptance or recognition which no longer serve you as an adult? These automatic responses and emotions may have surfaced time and again but you were not ready to uncover their foundation. Perhaps now is the time and this book is the opportunity for you to discover why your life is not unfolding the way you would like. Whether your desire is to find success in personal or public relationships, increased creativity, prosperity, motivation, physical health, healing of past childhood trauma, or to awaken spirituality, your own inner child can help guide you.

Jung tells us that the goal of the individuation process is the synthesis of the Self-uniting conscious and unconscious (subconscious), as well as, balancing body, mind and spirit. The techniques found in Re-Creation Therapy™ can help to revive and heal the unaware or subconscious elements. Each of these subconscious aspects retain outmoded belief systems, repressed emotions, predisposed illness, religious suppressions, and other blockages which can prevent us from achieving autonomy and wholeness.

On a physical level, to maintain a state of physical balance, or homeostasis, a constant flux of new cells replace the destruction of old cells. On the emotional/mental level, we keep our balance by "staying calm" and at the same time actively alert to our environment. On the spiritual level, we assume attunement with a Higher Power. These methods of maintaining a state of balance are usually accomplished unconsciously. They become conscious only when we *choose* to act and react from a level of awareness. Therefore, to bring a conscious awareness to each level—body, mind, and spirit—one's highest potential can be revealed.

On a physical level: During childhood we take into our bodies all the stress and emotional turmoil we experience and witness. Not understanding stress management or quiet healing time at this age, some claim we actually hold these negative elements from childhood in our cellular structure during our maturation. As we become adults much of these traumatic stresses are built upon until our bodies can cope no longer and a breaking down of cell structure results in illness. Working through childhood trauma can help release and heal the physical body and its trauma.

On the emotional/mental level: You may find that a great deal of the time you are oblivious to your thoughts and feelings, allowing them to wander aimlessly within the subconscious realm. However, it has been proven within the medical arena that "what" you think directly affects your physical health. Subscribers of positive thinking indicate that how we use our mental/emotional energies is directly related to how we experience our reality. If we *choose* to act and react consciously toward ourselves and others, we will stay in balance; however, if we *do not choose* but instead remain locked into subconscious mental and emotional patterns, we find ourselves entertaining frustration, discouragement, depression, confusion, unhappiness, fear, and the many other symptoms which accompany the imbalance of the conscious and subconscious mind. Taking responsibility for emotional health means being willing to *feel* even when afraid to do so.

On the spiritual level: Instilled within us before birth is an enlightened fragment of the Divine which can be consciously called upon for guidance at any time in our lives. However, even if not consciously activated this spiritual aspect remains hidden manifesting through intuitive glimpses, a sixth sense, and synchronistic events (coincidences which cannot be ignored). This spiritual nature is directly connected to the Child Within. As children we came into our lives with this purity of spirit, our inner child is the link. The process of Re-Creation Therapy™ and your own child within can unlock your subconscious mind to assist your remembrance of this true-Self.

The techniques of hypnosis and autohypnosis found in this book can liberate many of the hidden blockages and forgotten assets held tight in the subconscious. In his book, *Global Mind Change*, Willis Harman speaks of the phenomenon of hypnosis and the concept of reality:

> ...it is well established from research in hypnosis and other areas of experimental psychology that once a person has an internalized picture of reality, further experience tends to confirm that picture. Reality is experienced in accordance with the established picture, sometimes at the cost of gross perceptual distortion and elaborate rationalization to make it all hold together.

Rationalization is just one of the adapted techniques we employ to keep the picture of our reality alive and well. When we are challenged by new information from our environment often our first reaction is—from the internal subconscious—to review our past attempting to gain reassurance regarding our established picture. However, this picture is many times just an illusion of the true reality.

To demonstrate this *illusional reality* let me tell you how an elephant is trained in India. When an elephant is very young the trainer places a thick heavy rope around its leg and ties the other end to a secure post or tree. As the elephant matures and grows larger the trainer gradually reduces the size and weight of the rope. Finally, when full grown the elephant needs only a small flimsy strap tied to a short stub in the ground to become submissive and completely controlled. We humans construct our belief systems and our reality in this same manner.

As children we are very eager to please our elders whether parents, siblings, teachers, grandparents and other family members, or religious figures. We learn to adapt to imposed ideas, restrictions, mental and physical confinements, and various other commitments. We literally "take-in" our environment's offerings and tuck the entire package into the recesses of our subconscious minds. Then when this mindset is threatened with new assumptions or challenging opinions, we turn to our *illusional reality*, our ingrained structured beliefs. We unconsciously sort through them and arrive at what we think is the best determined conclusion based upon our past experience and previous assumptions. This outcome becomes our rationalized rope.

As unique individuals growing up in our exclusive childhoods, we formed an illusional reality structured from our particular environment. We, now as adults, live happily with our "rationalized ropes" of internalized beliefs, or do we? Harman elaborates:

> The fundamental fact, powerful and empowering
> in its implications, is that our experiencing of reality
> is strongly affected by our internalized beliefs.... each
> of us, from infancy onward, is subjected to a complex

set of suggestions from our social environment, which in effect teaches us how to perceive the world.... each of us is literally hypnotized from infancy to perceive the world the way people in our culture perceive it.... A prime task of adult life is to become dehypnotized, "enlightened"—to see reality as it is and to "know thy Self."

To "know thy Self" is a challenge for every adult. This is not an easy task for deep programming from childhood blocks a clear perception of the true-Self. To become dehypnotized and begin to see reality from your true-Self first requires the recognition of that Self. Your child within can bring you this gift. As an adult, you can relearn to choose the input you wish to experience and re-create childhood experiences and the emotions attached to them.

The ability to manifest the life you wish to experience is based upon your ability to unify what you believe you deserve and are capable of attaining with what you were *taught* you could be and possess while you were a child. You *can* reprogram your subconscious mind by replacing what was actually experienced with a more positive image. Only you can take a closer look at your past, your childhood, to discover what perceptions, beliefs, or illusional realities you want to change.

You possess all that is needed to heal yourself. You possess a creative mind, a physicality, and the spiritual nature which can direct you to your own child within guide. Your inner child is directly connected to that part of yourself which is complete and pure. Allow yourself to be guided. You can begin this inner journey by reaching for recovery.

2 Reaching for Recovery

"Return to the beginning;
Become a child again."
—Tao Te Ching

The first step in any recovery program is the self-awareness and self- acknowledgment surrounding an aspect of your life which is *not* working for you. In order for change to take place, first check to see what is *not* working in your reality—your interpersonal relationships, career, health, creativity. This self-awareness process tells you what must be altered or changed to encourage success. The acknowledgment that there *are* areas in your life in which you would like to grow is a giant step forward into healing and recovery. After acknowledging that you have an area of growth you want to develop or heal—that you feel lost, unsuccessful, filled with rage, lonely, "not quite right," uncreative, or just not "in balance"—you can reach for your child within to guide and direct you to the underlying foundations or reasons for your frustrations and concerns.

One important step in acknowledging how you feel is the action of "breaking the silence." Breaking the silence requires sharing openly and honestly with another person(s) about your present feelings and your childhood background which is influencing your present situation. This may be the first time you consider sharing this area of your life. Your emotions may range from guilt and shame to self-doubt and fear. However, if you choose to break the silence, you will experience a greater sense of self-awareness and support.

Choosing a suitable confidant with whom to share your feelings is important. You may wish to employ the aid of a trained counselor. The issue here is complete support and understanding for your feelings and childhood experiences. You may feel that sharing your woundedness is not appropriate at this time. Again, the choice is yours.

After you have discovered, acknowledged, and possibly shared some of the areas of your childhood which are holding you back in some fashion, you automatically begin to be more *self-aware*. What is self-awareness? It is the act of discovering who you are as a unique individual—without your parents' rules, religious belief systems, or your own self-imposed limitations employed for survival.

Jung spoke of an "individuation process" when referring to self-awareness and wholeness by stating the necessity for a person to integrate the unconscious (subconscious mind) with the conscious mind. By bringing direct awareness to your consciousness, you begin tearing down the infamous walls silently surrounding your true-Self. Poet René Char put it this way, "For those who are walled-up everything is a wall... even an open door." It is time to tear down these walls—the blockages of woundedness and imposed belief systems—and allow yourself to see the open door leading to recovery.

The True-Self

Once you allow yourself to begin to discover your true-Self, you will notice new doors opening to you. One client at this point in her recovery mentioned that she had never realized how she seemed "...to have a chip on (her) shoulder, needing to challenge everyone for everything." This is a typical self-awareness opening. It may sound small but this one discovery of self-awareness began this woman's healing and recovery process.

Janet, one of my former clients, was raised in a dysfunctional family with an overpowering mother who instilled in her a sense of worthlessness. As much as she tried to please her mother, Janet found she could never fulfill her mother's expectations. One incident Janet related occurred when she was between the ages of seven and twelve years old. One of Janet's household duties at this age was to clean the bathrooms in the house. She would work diligently scrubbing and cleaning only to have her mother criticize her efforts then commence to re-clean the rooms over again herself. This undermining of Janet's sense of accomplishment kept her continually trying harder to please her non-accepting mother.

Eventually, Janet stopped competing and chose instead to rebel against her mother, or any adult authority. The self-protective behavior Janet learned as a child turned her into a pushy defensive woman challenging most everyone she met. In her first few months of using the techniques of Re-Creation Therapy™, Janet recognized her self-defeating behaviors and attitudes and how they originated in her childhood. She realized each time she was challenged emotionally a "direct line to her childhood was triggered." This awareness gave Janet the personal power to stop her triggered behavior and replace it with a more suitable response.

Many times the subconscious mind works through dreams, fantasies, daydreams, or flashes of inspiration. If you recognize and acknowledge these insights, they can lead you to a greater capacity of self-awareness. Through this new found awareness you can embark upon a transition—a new beginning. Self-awareness can also be *triggered* by a present situation or emotion which originates from the past as in Janet's case. Bruce's story is also an example of this type of self-awareness breakthrough.

Bruce realized his life was not what he wanted it to be but was unable to put his finger on the reason. He felt empty, alone, and lost. He was studying to become a concert pianist and felt his creativity blocked and a sudden fear of performing. One day while practicing, he experienced a flashback of himself as a child sitting at his parent's piano just beginning to learn how to play. His father was cruel and told him he would never learn to play successfully. This insightful vision provided Bruce the self-awareness he needed to seek therapy and work through his negative childhood conditioning.

As Bruce began to explore his child within, he uncovered other painful experiences with his father. He was able to release much of the emotion attached to these memories during age regression techniques and re-create them into loving, positive events. He soon captured the self-acceptance and self-love he so deeply desired as a child. Bruce experienced a transforming awareness which provided an understanding of the reasons he felt so blocked in his creativity. He discovered how he had been holding onto his father's repeated assaults of displeasure and dissatisfaction with his choices in life which were subconsciously inhibiting him to pursue his lessons fully. This new found awareness gave Bruce a new foundation for self-acceptance and self-worth.

When you verbalize the need for direction and support as did Bruce and Janet, the steps toward recovery become visible. Your child within knows only too well the pain you suffered and is waiting patiently for you to tap into the powerful insight he or she possesses. Author and lecturer Stephen Levine has made a wonderful healing meditation CD entitled "Healing with Loving Kindness" which not only speaks of healing the pain and suffering of ourselves but of the entire planet. In the introduction, Levine poignantly relates, "Letting go of suffering is the hardest work we'll ever do and only you can do that work."

Reaching for recovery is a very personal journey. If at any time you feel the need to discuss your "travels" with another person, I recommend a therapist certified in Hypnotherapy to help guide you to your destination. The following steps for healing and recovery are guidelines found in Re-Creation Therapy™. Each of these seven steps are addressed throughout this book and are accompanied by various tools and exercises to facilitate your journey to recovery:

- Acknowledgment
- Self-Awareness
- Meeting your Child Within
- Emotional Release Exercises
- The Re-Creation Process
- For-Giving
- Letting Go

Reaching Steps

Recovery (healing) from being raised in a "dysfunctional" family environment may take many years of self-awareness and insight, as well as, a conscious effort to deal with the blockages and negative programming revealed by such awareness. Remember each small step forward will ultimately carry you to your goal. As you begin reaching for recovery many feelings will arise, one of which may be the sense that something is *wrong* with you. This assumption occurs often and many people delay seeking assistance because they feel embarrassed, guilty, or at fault—imposing a sense of shame upon themselves. It was traumatic for me to share my personal childhood experiences involving my father and his alcoholism and I will be on the road to recovery for many years. Be assured: We are all healing together.

Denial is another issue which may surface as you begin exploring the events, feelings, and thoughts which brought you to this stage in your life. Denial has been shown to be one of the main defense mechanisms found within the dysfunctional family system. It is a *survival* element. If it arises, examine it. Ask your inner most Self if this is the correct time in your life to delve into your past trauma. If you believe it would be beneficial for you to learn about your childhood beliefs, conditioning, and blockages, you can trust it is the right time to discover your child within.

In reaching for recovery with your inner child, you may begin to recognize the inner child of friends, relatives, parents, and coworkers. You may find yourself more objective about other's moods and responses. Examine your own mannerisms and emotional reactions. Do they stem from the child within? Many times, we hear ourselves saying things we really do not intend to say; or, saying things we do not believe in; or, repeat things that we have heard others say. Often our outbursts of emotion are based deep within us, ghosts from the past hidden in a mist of forgotten memories. By becoming more aware of this part of yourself—the child within you—you can more fully direct your actions and reactions from a place of adult maturity.

We have all received, at one time or another, a verbal or nonverbal attack from another person. As you delve into your own inner child's emotions, you will begin to understand from where these emotional attacks originate—the other person's inner child. When you learn *you* are not the cause for the emotional release of another person, it becomes easier to detach yourself emotionally and handle these conflicts from a place of understanding.

Lastly, when you allow yourself to experience your inner child, you will understand your desires, fears, self-imposed limitations, and your true-Self. You will begin to explore the many possibilities of a limitless existence as you recognize the intricacies of the child within. This existence holds life's fullest rewards, 1) Self-love and self-acceptance, and 2) A greater capacity to become oneself through the freedom of self-choice. You will *not* need to change your relationships, environment, or lifestyle to benefit from the gifts your inner child will bring you—or you may freely choose to change it all. You *can* create a happy successful present and future by re-creating past childhood trauma stored within your subconscious mind.

The child you once were (and the childhood you experienced) is the foundation for your present life as an adult. Every event, every emotion, every thought is recorded in detail within your subconscious mind. As an adult you may not consciously realize the affect your inner child has on your life; however, your motivations, lifestyle, personality, beliefs, weaknesses, values, habits, and strengths are all a product of how you perceived yourself, your world, and how you believed others perceived you during your childhood.

We create our reality from what we know and believe to be (belief precedes experience). We become what we *believe* ourselves to be. As an example, if we believe we are less than perfect, this image is held in our mind. If we are taught to hate and to mistrust others, this is exactly what we will experience. Conversely, if we are taught to love and feel we are successful, we will find these qualities within and around us. How are we taught these beliefs? We learn through our environment—parents, teachers, siblings, grandparents, religious figures. We, as children, learned well our limits and limitations while at the same time stuffing our little known true-Self deep within our hearts.

This true-Self is waiting to communicate with you. When you reach for him or her, you may remember many happy times or you might touch only the confusing, painful experiences. All of your childhood memories are important and learning to communicate with your child within requires only a few easy techniques.

Take a moment right now to take the first reaching steps toward meeting your child within. Close your eyes and reflect back on your childhood home. Perhaps there were several houses you lived in as a child—zero in on one. Now peek inside this house, see the different rooms, sense the emotional tone, and lay upon the bed where you slept. Open your eyes. Were you able to sense yourself back in time within that familiar house? How did you feel... happy, sad, angry, free, or strange as though you were not really there? Where is that part of yourself which lingers in the past?

Was it really necessary to become an adult and leave that feeling free child behind? Was it necessary to *replace* your inner child's wisdom and intuition with adult logic? Mastering rational thinking took you a step further from the freedom your inner child possesses. We become more logical and rational as society directs us, thus, we close off parts of our true-Self. This may have happened to you at an early age as you tried to "fit in" to your family's rules and belief systems. Whatever the age, did you adapt by shutting down the free inner child? Surrounded by rules and regulations—do's and don'ts—you may have become encased in an illusionary bubble. This personal surrender occurs quite unconsciously in childhood, however, at the high price of burying the spontaneous, intuitive, free child deep within.

If you had an extremely traumatic childhood—an alcoholic parent, incestuous relationship, or other physical, mental, or emotional abuse—the concept of relearning or re-creating a belief system may seem foreign to you because as a child it was necessary to adapt quickly without the luxury of weighing facts or circumstances. Children living in such an environment learn the systems of the family *without thinking* on their own to avoid initiating negative responses. Many times this type of survival behavior becomes maladaptive when continued into adulthood. However, if you were one of these children, you were unconsciously doing exactly what you needed to do to survive—and survive you did!

Rather than consciously struggling to *overcome* negative beliefs about yourself, you can reach for your inner child and discover the patterns and beliefs which you are still maintaining but have outgrown as an adult. Beginning to work with your inner child can be a rewarding experience much like opening a new door to a room you can fill with your own *chosen* feelings and thoughts. You can choose a more healthy self-image and re-create a new reality. For possibly the first time in your life, you can allow yourself the opportunity to consciously *choose* your life's path.

Listen to your inner child. He or she wants to be remembered. You have the opportunity through various exercises within this book to communicate with your own child within. Allow him or her to uncover all the fears and rigid rules locked in your subconscious mind so you can re-create them into strengths and values enabling you to live as a successful adult. There are many methods in the counseling field to help facilitate these initial steps toward healing. Whatever you choose to do to uncover your own inner child is *okay*. There are no wrong choices in self-discovery.

Several tools and techniques such as affirmations, art therapy, autohypnosis, visualizations, and other exercises are included at the end of each Chapter to guide you through the process of Re-Creation Therapy™. You may also wish to keep a daily or weekly Journal; this can be a private healing tool for your eyes only. Writing is a way of eliciting the subconscious—the intuitive part of your mind. Try jotting down your present feelings right now about reading this book. Not caring if words are spelled correctly or sentences are complete, allow yourself to let the feelings and thoughts flow. This is not an exercise in creative writing, rather an inside look at *who you are becoming.*

Also provided at the end of each Chapter are a few blank pages for you to continue writing your thoughts, feelings, and experiences. Let your Journal lead you to a sense of where you have begun and where you are traveling on your path to recovery. As you reread your Journal, are there specific words or images which trigger feelings from the past? Do you remember certain events or emotions from your childhood you are willing to explore? Your Journal can be an excellent measuring tool for your progress. There may even be a poem, fantasy, or fairytale locked within you! Many of my clients have been delighted when writing in their Journals, it inspired a deeper exploration and brought clarity to their emotions. If you enjoy writing, explore with pen in hand and perhaps you will uncover your own forgotten story.

Forgotten Stories

Remember the fable about a little boy trying to discover his true-Self? His name was Pinocchio. At the beginning of the story Pinocchio knew only his *false-self*. He was made of wood, unfeeling and rigid. His lack of emotion and compassion kept him locked into an illusional reality in which no one really knew him. Inside, Pinocchio felt he was "real" and alive but not even his father was aware of this inner spirit locked within his son. As the fable continues, Pinocchio becomes increasingly naughty, telling lies, skipping out on school lessons and soon finds himself among people he does not relate to or even like. Each time he is "untrue to himself" his nose grows longer and longer.

At this point in the story, a friend (his Higher-Self) in the form of a cricket enters Pinocchio's life. He chooses to ignore this confidant's wisdom and guidance continuing to be the "wooden head" his father proclaimed of him. Then one day Pinocchio is eaten by a large fish—a whale in some versions, a shark in others—and he finds himself in total darkness. This hidden place of darkness is an analogy for the subconscious mind. Pinocchio is faced with two choices. To escape his pretend life and choose to discover his true-Self; or, to remain forever in the dark. He ultimately escapes through a tunnel-like passage into the Light and reveals the "real" little boy he felt himself to be all along.

One well known author and therapist in the Adult Children of Alcoholics (ACoA) field is Jane Middelton-Moz. She introduces a fairy tale in her book, *Shame and Guilt: Masters of Disguise*, which actively describes the life experience of many people raised in a dysfunctional family environment. The tale is about a child named "Perfect" and her parents who are named "Giants." Perfect goes through life feeling guilty and ashamed because she can never live up to the Giant's expectations. Then one day she meets "Human Being." Human Being tells Perfect that she is *perfect* just the way she is and that being Human, not a Giant, is the destiny of her race.

Writing fictional stories while going through a therapy process is one of the most revealing methods to explore one's subconscious mind. It has been said that all great writers channel their material in an almost trancelike state allowing the inner (subconscious) mind to creatively guide their thoughts.

In the early 1800s there were two brothers, Jacob and Wilhelm Grimm, who wrote literally hundreds of fairy tales trying to enlighten the people of that era about personal, interpersonal, and social mores. Their personal and social concerns are woven into tales which still read like "innovative strategies for survival." These short stories with their "once upon a time" preludes help keep our own present day dreams alive for a better world. The following two Grimm tales may seem "grim" indeed, however, look closer at the underlying themes. As you read, reflect on the issues that arise for you and your own childhood.

"The Stubborn Child"
Once upon a time there was a stubborn child who never did what his mother told him to do. The dear Lord, therefore, did not look kindly upon him and let him become sick. No doctor could cure him, and in a short time he lay on his deathbed. After he was lowered into his grave and was covered over with earth, one of his little arms suddenly emerged and reached up into the air. They pushed it back down and covered the arm with fresh earth, but that did not help. The little arm kept popping out. So the child's mother had to go to the grave herself and smack the little arm with a switch. After she had done that, the arm

withdrew, and then, for the first time, the child had peace beneath the earth.

"The Three Lazy Sons"

Once upon a time a King had three sons, and since he loved them equally, he did not know which to choose to be king after his death. When the time of his death drew near, he summoned them to his bedside and said, "Dear children, I've been contemplating something for a while, and now I want to reveal it to you: I've decided that the laziest among you shall become king after me."

"Then, Father," said the oldest, "the kingdom belongs to me, for I'm so lazy that, when I'm lying on my back and want to sleep and a drop of rain falls on my eyes, I won't even shut them so I can fall asleep."

The second said, "Father, the kingdom belongs to me, for I'm so lazy that, when I'm sitting by the fire to warm myself, I'd sooner let my heels be burned than draw back my feet."

The third said, "Father, the kingdom is mine, for I'm so lazy that, if I were about to be hanged and the noose were already around my neck and someone handed me a sharp knife to cut the rope, I'd rather let myself be hanged than lift my hand to cut the rope."

When the father heard that, he said, "You've outdone the others and shall be king."

(The above examples are chosen so you might learn how to acknowledge your *own* pain; however, your childhood story certainly may not be as grim or negative.)

In the first Grimm tale many of you can identify with the hidden messages. *Hidden* is the key word. There are hidden messages that if the child did not satisfy the wishes of others he would be punished. There are also hidden agreements that he keep silent, never to reach out and ask for his needs to be met. This little child was surely forced to hide his true-Self forever.

The second tale reflects the outrageous ways in which we try to follow our parents' wishes, even to the detrimental degree of sacrificing our own life. It demonstrates to what lengths we are willing to go in the attempt to receive parental love. People have been known to even develop the same illnesses as their parents as a way to subconsciously show loyalty and receive love from them. Exercise #3 at the end of this Chapter offers guidance on how to begin writing your own childhood fable. This exercise may elicit deep emotions from your childhood memories. Many of my clients and students have successfully used personal childhood fable-writing to begin the unraveling of their past trauma.

In reaching for your child within, you may wish to literally travel to the town and surroundings in which you grew up. This may not be possible for many, however, *all* can visit their childhood environment through the use of self-guided imagery. This tool is readily available to everyone. Take a moment to try the following exercise. Read the entire passage below then put down this book and enlist your subconscious mind to follow the directions.

> Close your eyes and get totally comfortable. Allow yourself to breathe deeply with a few cleansing breaths.... Feel your body begin to relax, each muscle going limp and soft. When you are completely relaxed, sense the room filled with helium balloons floating over your head. Each bright colored balloon has a number printed on it. The numbers range from one to ten. Checking each colorful balloon—read the numbers clearly. One of those numbers stands out more boldly than the rest and your attention is drawn directly to it.... Totally focusing your attention on this one balloon let the number on it stay with you as the balloon descends to you. Easily picture yourself at the *age* of the printed number and in the surroundings where you grew up at that time. Sense your small bodyframe, your thoughts and your emotions as a child. Listen for familiar sounds in your house and smell the lingering scents. Touch the bed coverings of your bed and see the colors in your

room. Stay with the image for approximately two to three minutes.... Gradually return fully awake, alert, remembering every detail of your experience.

Experiencing the above technique allows you to experiment with autohypnosis and visualization to experience yourself as a child. Were you able to visualize the balloons with the numbers on them? Could you picture yourself at the chosen age? This may be the first time in a long while that you have even thought about yourself at the chosen age. Did any feelings arise that you had not felt in a long time? Whatever your experience with this exercise, you did it right! Wherever you are on your road to healing and recovery, *you* are the expert. Follow your *own inner guidance* to which steps to take next and how far to go.

Learning autohypnosis, or venturing into a therapy which uses hypnosis, can be rewarding and challenging at the same time. Give yourself permission right now to leap a step further to work with the following exercises and reach for recovery. The amount of energy and time you invest will depend upon your individual needs at the present. Repeat the exercises you choose. Repetition is essential in gaining the desired healing and recovery you are seeking from your inner child. It took many years to be molded into the person you are today, take the time to re-create your beliefs and behaviors and allow yourself to accept these gifts from *your* child within.

Child Within Exercises

1. To help you reach and remember your childhood, thumb through your old childhood photographs. Allow the memories of yourself as a child to flow spontaneously. Focus on the pictures from these times past and bring each one to your conscious mind. As you look at each picture, visualize yourself at that age. Get in touch with the little boy or little girl within you. Let this short poem, written by a young girl, inspire you to search for the old photographs buried in the closet drawer.

> thumbed portraits
> worn corners
> the pictures taken every year
> stuffed in the file cabinet
> of the library of memories
> the last clues
> to the child within.
>
> Jenny Lee, age 9
> Corte Madera, CA

2. Re-experience childhood activities. Go out and fly a kite; take a hike; go fishing; play ball; dig in the dirt or sand; choose any childhood activity which you enjoyed. You might also buy yourself a child's toy, stuffed animal, or crayons and coloring book to encourage your inner child to awaken within you. If you are physically unable to experience these activities, visualize yourself experiencing the wonderfully free and agile movements of your youth. Imagine yourself riding a merry-go-round; petting a puppy; rolling down a grassy hill; or swinging on a swing. Participating in an event which you did as a child helps to connect the subconscious memories and feelings with your conscious adult awareness.

3. In a quiet private place take out a piece of paper and pen. Close your eyes, take a few deep breaths to relax your body and mind. Focus on yourself as a young child. Allow yourself to run a movie in your mind of your growing up years. See the story unfold frame by frame. When you are ready to write hold the pen in your non-dominate hand and

write the beginning words, "Once upon a time there was a child born...." After a few sentences return the pen to your dominate writing hand and allow the storyteller within you to finish the tale of your forgotten child within.

Remember, this is a fable, a fairy tale seeded with Truths. Your story is not intended for others to read if you do not wish to share it. Let yourself tell the story of a time long ago when your child within lived, laughed, cried, felt afraid, and longed for affection. Make it real. Be creative, write in the details of your childhood traumas as you felt and experienced them as a child. When your fairy tale is complete, read it over carefully. Allow yourself time to remember that little child within you. When you feel ready, read and experience the following Child Within Autohypnosis.

Child Within Affirmations

At the end of each Chapter is a separate page for positive affirmations. An affirmation is a powerful tool. It is a statement of truth which overrides negative thinking. Read each one aloud several times—feel its potency—then take a few minutes to write your own affirmations. Write simple, positive, present tense sentences such as, "I am becoming more and more aware of my child within each day."

The following affirmation was written in the "Daily Word" magazine which is published by Unity Village located in Missouri:

I AM PROGRESSING IN A POSITIVE DIRECTION

From whatever point I am experiencing life now, I can make a positive move toward greater fulfillment. Whatever type of person I now seem to be, I can begin to grow into the person that God created me to be.... I can choose a new pattern of thinking and acting that will bring me greater joy and inner peace.

If I am unhappy with the way I have reacted in some circumstance, I have the power to change my own behavior. I have an inner spark of divinity, the spiritual me that has been created in the image and likeness of God[/Goddess/All That Is]. It is the perfection of this likeness that I wish to express in the outer.

I turn to inner guidance so that I think, speak, and act positively.

I follow a higher calling, and move at a comfortable pace in a positive direction.

Add your own Child Within Affirmations:

I accept my inner child as a part of myself.

I reach for my inner child by staying open to all my emotions.

I invite my child within to share his/her gifts with me.

Child Within Autohypnosis

Relax and breathe deep the silence. Go within and find a quiet space, a place of stillness to call your own. Create the special setting in your mind's eye—a pond of clear blue water, a mountain's peak, a private meadow, or a favorite secluded beach.

Visualize yourself strolling among the beauty of this special place. On your journey you feel the sun's warmth pressing against your back and the wind's coolness dancing in your hair. You have indeed created a perfect space in time.

On your walk you notice a small child in the far distance. Who is this child you wonder as you draw near. When you are a few feet away the child turns to face you. You are a bit startled to see this child is *you*. How curious it is to see this small face again, this younger-self you thought you had left behind. At first you cannot help but stare, not knowing quite what to do. In a moment's time, you buildup the courage and reach out your hand knowing only you can begin this bonding. Allow your feelings to direct your actions—perhaps the two of you hug and share, or maybe just sitting in silence is what feels best. *Visualize this moment as only you can.*

When you are ready to leave, your inner child will have something to say and/or give to you. Listen carefully and remember this important message or gift. Though this first encounter with your inner child may be brief, know that you can always return to your special place and touch your inner child with love.

Child Within Journal

As I am hugging my Child Within, She whispers in my ear that everything is going to be okay. That I am worth it and that I am loved. That it is okay to be myself.

Child Within Journal

3   The Process of
Re-Creation Therapy™

> In every adult there lurks a child—an eternal
> child, something that is always becoming,
> is never completed, and calls for unceasing
> care, attention, and education.
> That is the part of the human personality
> which wants to develop and become whole.
> —C.G. Jung

A process is "a systematic series of actions marked by gradual changes that lead toward a particular result." The process found in Re-Creation Therapy™ is characterized by gradual changes in self-awareness which lead to a greater understanding of the psychodynamics the child within plays in the adult life. The end result is the beginning of the transformative steps found in Jung's individuation process. These steps become evident as you begin living a more consciously creative life with a sense of new found freedom, the *power of choice.*

Within the process of Re-Creation Therapy™ is the total adventure of reaching, meeting, exploring and releasing emotions, re-creating circumstances and feelings, and healing the child within. It includes a series of exercises enabling you to strengthen the bond between you and your inner child. These methods assist your ability to learn from your many childhood experiences (both positive and negative). They pinpoint exactly where and why you may be sabotaging yourself with old belief patterns. You may find some of the methods more helpful than others. Select the techniques that work best for *you* and enjoy discovering the magic of your child within.

The success of Re-Creation Therapy™ is based upon the working relationship between the conscious mind and the subconscious mind. Nearly 88% of our actions throughout our lives are directed by our subconscious mind. This subconscious aspect of our being does not think or make decisions. It does not know right from wrong, good from bad, reality from illusion. The subconscious only follows directions. These directions, or programs, are accepted and stored much as a computer stores the input typed into it. Where does the subconscious get this information? It receives all its data from *you*—both consciously and unconsciously.

A picture formed in the brain derived by what you are sensing, feeling, seeing, hearing, and thinking, is sent directly to the subconscious mind where it immediately is recorded and stored until called upon. Emotions energize this picture, they make the image more potent. It does not matter to the subconscious whether this picture (and the emotions attached to it) is negative or positive. The process remains the same. The subconscious mind receives any and every detail of information surrounding your life from birth (possibly from the womb and beyond) and this input is conveniently hidden from view until appropriately retrieved.

This stored data can be difficult to alter and at times almost impossible to retrieve; however, it is necessary to change, transform, or re-create the material held in the subconscious to complete the maturation process. Can you imagine what you would be like now as an adult if you did not relearn, or reprogram some of the opinions and scripts you possessed as a child? It would be foolish to assume we never change our beliefs.

We all have outdated beliefs and feelings which suited us as children but are no longer appropriate. One such opinion comes to mind about adults "kissing." When I was about five years old, I remember thinking how awful kissing must be between two grownups. How could they touch each other's lips and tongues together? Ugh! However, I changed this belief quite rapidly in my teenage years of experimentation. Now as an adult, I am certainly glad I did!

To change or transform a tightly held subconscious pattern requires motivation, determination, and patience. The script must be consciously brought to the surface; the attached emotions released; then both the script and its emotions re-created to fit the present adult reality. To accomplish this, Re-Creation Therapy™ techniques employ hypnosis—either autohypnosis or with the guidance of a Hypnotherapist.

The subconscious mind does not distinguish between reality and illusion. Research has proven that what we imagine or visualize is accepted by our mind/brain just as if we had actually experienced the event. To make this point, close your eyes and think of a juicy, tart yellow lemon. Now take a knife and cut this succulent fruit in half and smell the sourness of its juice. Put the lemon close to your lips and let a drop of liquid touch your tongue. Now open your eyes. Could you almost taste your imagined lemon? This exercise demonstrates how powerful our visualizing abilities and mind power are when we focus our attention. Hypnosis (and autohypnosis) work with the mind in this same manner.

Hypnosis is an altered state of consciousness. It lies between the awake "beta" state of consciousness and the sleeping "delta" state. The states of consciousness called "alpha" and "theta" are the in-between states in which one is either daydreaming, just about to fall asleep, or just beginning to awaken. These in-between states of consciousness make up approximately ten minutes of every ninety-minute period that one is not asleep. When one is in this natural state of relaxation, it becomes very easy to direct or stimulate the subconscious mind.

Hypnotherapy is a form of therapy combining the trance induction of hypnosis with individual techniques of counseling. Therefore, Hypnotherapy cannot be precisely defined for every Hypnotherapist has specialized tools, techniques, and backgrounds specifically acquired from diverse counseling fields. Hypnotherapy encompasses a holistic approach to health and healing, looking at the total person and addressing not only the mind and emotions but the body and spiritual nature as well.

Hypnotherapist and author Gil Boyne, former Executive Director of the American Council of Hypnotist Examiners states, "Hypnotherapy is a naturalistic approach that uses the client's present resources and strengths to further and accomplish meaningful goals." As such, Hypnotherapy attempts to help clients to help themselves. Whatever the situation or process, says Boyne, Hypnotherapy is presented as "a dramatically rapid intervention system which strengthens and reshapes the client's feelings of competence and capability." One of the most important outcomes derived from using autohypnosis or undergoing Hypnotherapy is the realization that you have control over and can manifest your own reality.

That we create (or at the very least *affect*) our own reality is becoming more evident in current scientific thought. We are today what we have thought, acted upon, reacted to, and believed ourselves to be. We are the sum total of our experiences, perceptions, and beliefs. Within the process of Re-Creation Therapy™ you are guided toward many of these hidden beliefs and emotions, experiences and patterns which are defining your reality. If any of these perceptions are unwanted in your present, you can choose to re-create them thereby shaping a reality by conscious choice, not mere acceptance of what you believed you must accept. It is a *process* of self-awareness, conscious choice, and transformation. This "consciousness of self" is one of the highest rewards found within this healing process.

In his book, *Transforming Therapy*, Boyne states that the use of Hypnotherapy is always directed toward health and wholeness, toward an "inner grace." We can begin to touch this inner grace as we turn inward to the part of ourselves known perhaps only to the child within us. Roberto Assagioli, an Italian psychiatrist and creator of a holistic therapy called Psychosynthesis had his clients use hypnosis and imagery to help them connect with their inner grace. He has reported, "You can trust your deepest being and learn to live from that place. The *real* you knows all that you need to know, knows the future, will lead you." Assagioli asserts that the connection with the real self (true-Self) is a true link to that inner grace and wholeness we all seek.

Natural and Technical Transformation

Jung talked of individuation, the "natural transformation" of consciousness. In his writings *The Archetypes and the*

Collective Unconscious, Jung explains there are two forms of self transformation, "There are natural transformation processes which simply happen to us, whether we like it or not, and whether we know it or not and there are technical transformations."

Many times accompanying "natural transformations" is an acknowledgement of an inner grace, an inner friend which has been there all along but is now recognized. Jung calls this our "inner friend of the soul... This *other being* is the other person in ourselves—that larger and greater personality maturing within us, whom we have already met as the inner friend of the soul." The child within *is* this inner friend of the soul, your true-Self.

Jungian analyst Marion Woodman touches our acknowledgement of this inner friend of the soul—the child within—when writing about the feelings of abandonment many of us experienced in childhood:

> If we have lived behind a mask all our lives, sooner or later—if we are lucky—that mask will be smashed. Then we will have to look in our mirror at our own reality. Perhaps we will be appalled. Perhaps we will look into the terrified eyes of our own tiny child, that child who has never known love and who now beseeches us to respond. This child is alone, forsaken before we left the womb, or at birth, or when we began to please our parents and learned to put on our best performance in order to be accepted. As life progresses, we may continue to abandon our child by pleasing others—teachers, professors, bosses, friends and partners, even analysts. That child who is our very soul cries out from under the rubble of our lives, often from the core of our worst complex, begging us to say, 'You are not alone. I love you.'

Abandonment issues arise frequently in our search for acceptance and love. If you were literally abandoned by a parent (or parental figure) through desertion, death, or divorce, most likely you possess strong feelings of "rejection." To feel rejected by those you love is one of the most traumatic emotions one can experience. Even if your parents did not physically leave you but you still felt a sense of "not being heard or understood" as a child, feelings of abandonment or loneliness may persist as an adult.

Beverly, one of my past clients, was abandoned early in her life. At the age of ten her mother died of breast cancer and left Bev with a feeling of a "hole in the chest." As a child she had felt she was the *cause* of her mother's death because she had accidentally jabbed her mother in the breast which was later diagnosed with cancer. She did not share her fear and guilt with others but instead tried very hard to be "a good girl" and do everything she was told by her father. About a year later Bev's father died which accentuated her guilt and feelings of abandonment. She was sent to live with an older brother and his wife.

At this point in Beverly's life she understood death intellectually but not on an emotional level. She had not yet completely grieved for the loss of her mother for whom she still felt guilty and responsible. With both her parents "abandoning" her, Bev felt more than ever that she was at fault and needed to be "perfect" in order for others, anyone, to love her and not leave—abandon her.

During her therapy sessions, Beverly was able to acknowledge and release her inner child's anger surrounding her parents' death. While in age regression, she chose to re-create her inner child expressing the guilt she felt and began relating her feelings of abandonment. Also, Beverly acknowledged her continuing pattern of trying to be "Miss Perfect" in most areas of her life.

This process helped Beverly discover the hidden reasons for not being able to stay in a healthy relationship as an adult; why she felt *everything was her fault*; and how her feelings of abandonment were still directing her choices in life. By meeting and working with her "inner friend of the soul"—her child within—Beverly was able to re-create her childhood trauma of guilt and abandonment and move forward into recovery.

Jung explains that a natural transformation is not intentionally instigated while a "...technical transformation [requires] special techniques in which... the personal endeavor of the initiate is needed in order to achieve the intended purpose. It is a transformation experience induced by technical means." These technical methods can range from simple imagery to the use of a prescribed drug-induced trance. Technical transformations can be associated with many holistic or alternative health methods resurging today. Some of these include biofeedback, bodywork, autogenic training, and acupuncture. The autohypnosis and/or Hypnotherapy methods found in Re-Creation Therapy™ are transformative tools which initiate technical transformation as described here by Jung.

Milton Erickson, one of those who paved the way for the broad acceptance of Hypnotherapy, personally experienced technical transformation through the healing techniques of autohypnosis. While suffering from polio as a child he was left partially paralyzed and confined to a wheel chair. Because of his inability to move around, he began developing a keen eye for details. He would sit and listen to others for hours studying their every movement, expression, gesture, and tone of voice. He learned to utilize his innate intuition and acute concentration to the fullest extent.

Erickson soon discovered he was able to control his daily pain with mind control—what we now understand as autohypnosis. He transformed his pain into numbness which enabled him to endure the necessary long-term physical rehabilitation which returned him to his health. He evolved into what has been termed the "wounded healer" which creates a successful and compassionate therapist.

Literally, Erickson experienced and demonstrated what he later defined: "Hypnotic psychotherapy is a learning process for the patient, a procedure of reeducation." He always felt his *patient's* desired results were the only point to consider and that "how to guide constitute the therapist's problem while the patient's task is that of learning through his own efforts to understand his experiential life in a new way."

These parameters of counseling constitute the basis of Re-Creation Therapy™.

Erickson was under the impression that "the clinical practice of Hypnotherapy is currently emerging from a period of relative quiescence into an exciting time of new discoveries and fascinating possibilities." Hypnosis is now becoming accepted as a viable means of employing therapeutic methods during counseling. Hypnotherapists can deal directly with the inner child to reveal issues of abandonment, shame, emotional or physical abuse, and a myriad of inhibitors blocking a healthy persona.

Hypnotherapists who use processes like Re-Creation Therapy™ direct their client to *re-create the negative or traumatic experiences of childhood into what the client would have desired to have occurred.* Where common dialogue psychotherapy leaves off, Re-Creation Therapy™ just begins. Psychotherapy tends to propound that once the client has released the troubling emotions he/she can begin recovery. However, there is often a feeling of "emptiness" after purging oneself of traumatic emotions, a feeling of relief accompanied by one of fear regarding the unfamiliar territory which ensues. To fill this "void" or as Beverly so aptly termed it, "a hole in the chest," a positive re-creation of the emotion, event, or belief can encourage the client to restructure a new mode of feeling and thinking. In this way, the subconscious mind is aligned with the adult conscious mind.

It may appear as though the subconscious and conscious are two separate minds, however, there is only one mind. This mind contains the conscious, rational field *and* the subconscious or intuitive, hidden aspects. Bringing some of the subconscious thoughts and beliefs to the conscious mind's attention marks the onset of *self-awareness.* Following this self-awareness, one can re-create new patterns of behavior, events and emotions, or construct belief systems to form a more positive frame of reference for the present and future.

Some of the newer therapies using hypnosis (or guided imagery) today enlist the use of age regression techniques but fail to "fill the void" after the emotions have been released. Thus, there can be a hollowness or emptiness that lingers but is not quite understood by the client. When this happens, clients find themselves lacking the needed direction and support for which they entered therapy in the first place. It is important to replace the emotions of fear, doubt, shame, guilt, humiliation, abandonment, and so forth which are brought to the surface in therapy with ones of confidence, self-worth and self-esteem, the power of control and choice, and forgiveness of self and others. When the void which is left by the releasing of repressed emotions is filled, the client begins to feel and accept a sense of direction toward healing and recovery.

Author Adelaide Bry brings us another process of contacting the child within in her book *Visualization: Directing the Movies of Your Mind*. With the use of visualization, she focuses attention on challenging the client to "remember the way things *really* were when you were growing up." Then with different "movies-of-the-mind" she evokes realistic images to introduce the client to the inner child. This can be a truly successful beginning method to discover, meet, and learn about your child within. Bry writes, "Just as you would do when you watch a scary movie in a movie theater, simply watch it and feel whatever feelings it brings up, knowing that they will pass. When you are willing to look at the uncomfortable picture, it often changes into something happier by itself."

However, the *possibility* of change into "something happier" is not sufficient to re-program the subconscious or to reassure the conscious mind—there must be a re-creation, a reprogramming on a subconscious level of the undesired events or emotions. Processes using Re-Creation Therapy™ provide this necessary element. They also establish a supportive space to help initiate the emotions connected to your woundedness; help you sort through and release unwanted feelings; and they provide the guidance (via the Child Within) to re-create undesired experiences and emotions to fill the resultant void. You are given complete control over your healing and recovery.

You may choose to begin the process of Re-Creation Therapy™ without a therapist. You can initiate your healing and recovery by following the exercises, suggestions, and guidance found in this text. However, if you choose to have a therapist guide you through this process, choose one with experience in hypnosis and age regression. Theoretical understanding is not enough when it pertains to your emotional and mental health. As author and psychoanalyst Alice Miller noted, "Only therapists who have had the opportunity to experience and work through their own traumatic past will be able to accompany patients on the path to truth about themselves and not hinder them on their way." As a caution, if you decide to work with a therapist, ask him or her to share any past experience they have acquired in this area and if they employ the required hypnotic age regression in their counseling methods.

Guided Visualization

Re-Creation Therapy™ uses many methods to ensure Jung's "technical transformation" concept. In conjunction with hypnosis, guided visualization is employed. While under the influence of a hypnotic trance, guided visualization can be profound and revealing; however, you can easily use autohypnosis and receive nearly these same results. If you have chosen to begin your process without the aid of a therapist, you may wish to record the visualizations in your own voice to encourage the greatest benefit visualization can offer.

Visualization is an experience of the inner mind—it is just like seeing except it is done with the mind's eye or imagination using that part of the brain which registers thought, memory, ideas, and the subjective rather than the objective physical eye. Visualization can be used for the purpose of influencing both external and internal conditions. This technique is an effective means to communicate with the child within. It is a powerful transformative tool when used to re-create negative childhood trauma into positive experiences.

Some people have difficulty actually visualizing an image in their mind. If you find this to be true, try "sensing" the vision with your other sensory perceptions. There may be smells or sounds which accompany a memory or emotion; perhaps you can sense a color, texture, or hot/cold sensation. If you were able to imagine yourself meeting your inner child in the exercise at the end of Chapter Two you are well on you way to enlisting visualization in your healing process.

In her best seller *Creative Visualization*, Shakti Gawain defines creative visualization as "…. magic in the truest and highest meaning of the word." She continues to fully explain its dynamics:

> [Visualization] involves understanding and aligning yourself with the natural principles that govern the workings of our universe, and learning to use these principles in the most conscious and creative way.
>
> If you had never seen a gorgeous flower or a spectacular sunset before, and someone described one to you, you might consider it to be a miraculous thing (which it is!). Once you saw a few yourself, and began to learn something about the natural laws involved, it would seem natural to you and not particularly mysterious.
>
> The same is true of the process of creative visualization. What at first might seem amazing or impossible to the very limited type of education our rational minds have received, becomes perfectly understandable once we learn and practice with the underlying concepts involved.
>
> Once you do so, it may seem that you are working miracles in you…and you truly will be!

One of my clients, while working with Re-Creation Therapy™ visualized himself as a child running in the sand at the ocean. He felt so free of the worries which brought him into therapy during this vision that he decided to actually experience the event. He journeyed to the ocean and let himself fully feel the freedom of his inner child. Upon returning to his next session, he explained his experience and felt it was an opening of self-realization and shared how "locked in" he had been to his childhood beliefs of limitation.

Our self-imposed limitations can manifest as "lack consciousness"—when we think there cannot be enough of something to go around—not enough money, good jobs, love and so on. Our limitations can also be more personal such as a limiting fear, doubt, self-confidence, creative ability, and the list is *limitless!* The channeled entity Emmanuel speaks of the limitations we humans impose upon ourselves, "When the child is given alphabet blocks, he is given infinite possibility of communication. When he is taught the concepts of spelling, he is given limitation." Our ability for expanded thinking is many times halted by the limitations of structure and compliance.

One psychotherapist who uses guided visualization has his clients imagine a large door in front of them. On this door he instructs them to clearly see a word carved into it. The word represents a limitation and is chosen earlier, usually by the client. It can reflect a limitation such as fear, anger, loneliness, poverty, anxiety, or depression. At this point, the client is led through the doorway into a scene depicting the chosen word. Often the client will retrieve a past childhood memory when visualizing this scene, one perhaps of his parents fighting or himself as a child in an unpleasant situation.

This exercise can bring insight to why you feel limited or how a self-imposed limitation is overriding your life. Take a moment to try this exercise and allow any "blockages" of self-limitation to be revealed to you. Remember that whatever you visualize is *okay*. After completing the exercise take a few minutes to jot down in your Journal what you experienced. Which limiting blockage was imprinted on the door? Did a childhood experience come into the scene on the other side of the door? How does the word you chose reflect the visualization you experienced?

The first time I tried "the door" technique the word *SELF-CONFIDENCE* was carved into a huge oak door. When I opened the door, there was what appeared to be a bottomless pit. There was no way to get to the other side but I tried to side-step along the rim anyway. Suddenly, I decided to jump into it! I did not crash to the bottom as I feared but gently floated down a lighted tunnel arriving in the backyard of a house I had lived in from five to eleven years old. I was observing myself as a child hiding out in my cardboard playhouse which was surrounded in tall grasses. I felt safe but lonely and sensed a feeling of wanting attention but not knowing how to ask for it. I stayed with this image a few minutes then easily let it go and opened my eyes.

Reflecting back on my experience with this exercise, I understood immediately where my feelings of a lack of self-confidence had originated. These self-limiting feelings stemmed from my childhood experiences of not being given enough positive praise and attention. I began connecting phases and emotions to my life such as "hiding out;" not risking or putting myself "on the line" or feeling accepted for who I was; and feeling a true sense of inner loneliness. I used autohypnosis to relax my body and mind and slowly began to instruct myself to connect with my hurt child within. Repeatedly, I envisioned myself as a small child surrounded by family and friends who lavished attention and praise on my efforts to complete childhood tasks like drawing and coloring, crafts, and participating in games. I did this re-creation exercise often allowing my child within to truly feel how proud my parents were of me. I began feeling my self-confidence from the *inside*.

All of the insights this exercise gave me helped re-create my feelings of limitation. I discovered a new balance of self-awareness and self-confidence which awakened me to see my *limitless reality*.

Emmanuel continues to elaborate on our self-imposed limitations and the resultant illusional reality that follows this kind of restricted self-acceptance:

> You are all ensnared in illusion, much as if you were walking through a field of brambles. You entered the field, called by the beautiful wild flowers there. As you began to walk, to pick the joys, the beauties of this world, you found yourselves more and more entangled in the thorns, until you became so focused on the thorns that you quite forget why

you went into the field at all..... As children you have played at putting your hands in front of a bright light and watching the shadow figures on the wall. This is a clear analogy of your life. Do you choose to look at the shadows on the wall and say, "This is reality," or are you also aware of how those shadows were created and of the brilliant Light that stands behind all illusion?

Not only are you the shadow
that is dancing on the wall,
but you are the hand
that makes the shadow,
and you are the
Light.

Child Within Exercises

1. Set aside some quiet time so you will not be interrupted for about twenty minutes. In your Journal, or on a separate piece of paper, draw a vertical line down the middle. On the left side of the line at the top of the paper write your Mother's first name and on the right side write your Father's first name. Take a moment to get relaxed. Take three deep breaths closing your eyes and visualize your mother as you remember her while growing up. Think of her with your mind and with your feelings.

Now open your eyes and write under her name all the individual words that come to you such as busy, loving, lonely, rude, angry. Don't think too long—just jot them down quickly. When you feel completed with the list under your mother's name, again close your eyes, relax and imagine your father while you were a child. Complete the list under his name with the individual words which come to you. (If you were raised by people other than your parents, substitute their names at the top of the paper.)

Once again, close your eyes, relax your body/mind and think back about your family as a unit. What were the "rules" of the house? Most families have "unwritten" rules which govern its members such as "Never bother Daddy when he's in the garage" or "Don't talk to Mom when she's drinking." These rules are generally kept in silence by the family and are not discussed with outsiders. The spoken rules of a family can be just as harsh or limiting as the nonverbal ones, such as "You had better get good grades in school or you'll end up like your father" or "Don't touch yourself *down there*, that's dirty." At the bottom of your paper write some of the family rules which you remember from your childhood.

Next, go back up to the mother/father lists and read each one carefully. Afterward, put an "x" by the words in your lists which you can identify as being an aspect of yourself *now as an adult.* We tend to adopt many of the same traits and habits of our parents. It can be amazing to us when we first recognize the different ways in which we emulate those who raised us. Also, check your family rules list—what kinds of rules and limitations do you still impose upon yourself that were initiated in your childhood?

If during this self-discovery exercise, you find you have adopted a few traits, emotions, habits, or limiting "rules" which your parents possessed but you no longer wish to keep, you can learn to re-create each one of them allowing yourself to be your true-Self, not the mere shadow of your parents' lives. Do this slowly allowing yourself sufficient time to re-create every feeling and/or trait you wish to change. The next Child Within Autohypnosis can be used to enlist your child within to reveal the experience of each limiting aspect you wish to alter.

2. In this Chapter the "door" technique was presented. Try this exercise once more but first reflect on a particular trait or feeling which you acquired in your childhood. This may be a feeling which had not been recognized until now or one which you have consciously kept hidden for many years. When flying in a plane one's perspective or depth perception becomes confused. What looks like inches of land below is miles; what appears to be tiny green spots are in reality huge trees. Do not misjudge the power you possess within your own mind. What seems to be a fixed, non-changeable attitude or habit in reality is only a belief ready to be altered or re-created. *Name* your emotions, goals, habits, doubts, and so forth by carving the word into a door that you can open and *break the silence.*

> Once again relax and breathe deep the silence. Choose the word, feel the surrounding emotions and sense where they first stemmed in your childhood. Visualize yourself as a child and allow him or her to direct you to the door with the word carved into it. Open the door and experience the scene which follows. Take your time experiencing this vision. When you feel complete with the scene, keep your eyes closed and reflect upon the implications and awareness it brought you. You may feel the need to cry, shout, or hit a few pillows—release any emotions tied to the event. Finally, open your eyes and let go of your thoughts, relax your body. Take three deep

breaths to clear any residual emotions. Once again close your eyes and allow yourself to reenter the scene which you just experienced. If there are aspects which you or your child within would like to re-create, you can do so in your mind's eye. Continue using your powerful mind power to re-create the past event and emotions into what you would have liked to have happened. Search for the positive outcome and feelings you want by asking your child within to tell you what he or she desires. The beginning steps in Re-Creation Therapy™ are to recognize what you want to change. If, in your scene, you found an undesired emotion or event, use the power of your mind to re-create it.

Once you have completed the re-creation, open your eyes and feel the positive flow of energy radiating from within you. Look closer at the re-created scene you have unwrapped and discover the gifts of transformation your child within has given you and write them in your Journal.

Child Within Affirmations

I change my inner perception so the outer reveals the obscured beauty.

I concentrate on my inner vision and find my outer view transformed.

I have the power to change my behavior and emotions.

My child within guides me to the positive outcomes I desire.

Child Within Autohypnosis

Choose one of the traits or characteristics from the list you made in Exercise #1 which you desire to alter or change. While sitting in a comfortable position, close you eyes and concentrate on your chosen word. Allow yourself to breathe deeply for a few minutes to balance and center yourself. Begin thinking about the parent who possesses the trait or characteristic which you have chosen to re-create within yourself. What is it that makes this trait distasteful in that parent? When did you begin to recognize this characteristic in your parent? How did you acquire this trait or emotion? At what age? Why do you want to re-create this for yourself?

(Listen to your answers and reasons to the above questions as you explore deeper and deeper into your subconscious mind.)

When you feel firm and secure with your choice to re-create this trait, characteristic, or emotion, clear your mind. Picture yourself in your mind's eye at your present age facing the parent which possesses the trait you no longer wish to emulate. Gently, but firmly, tell your parent face to face that you are re-creating this aspect of yourself into a more desirable characteristic. *Name* the emotion, trait, or characteristic you are re-creating, then *name* the new one replacing it. Tell your parent you do not need to continue being or using this trait any longer to gain his/her approval or love. When you feel ready, open your eyes.

Affirm the new characteristic or emotion you have re-created by sharing it with another as soon as you feel ready. You may wish to write in your Journal about your experience at this point. Allow a few days before enlisting this autohypnosis for another word on your list of parental traits which you have subconsciously adopted. Give yourself a little time to consciously incorporate your new chosen characteristic or emotion. Remember it took several years to acquire it, be patient with yourself and take your time in re-creating it.

Child Within Journal

Child Within Journal

I have had an angery attitude for many years. Entitlement issues for sure. I remember my dad always yelling at my mom. Even if she had a different opinion than him. Even if a cup was left on the table, he would get very angry and verbally abuse us. I choose today to break the anger cycle and live a more peaceful and joyful life. I used to believe that I would never be good enough, or that something was very wrong with me. I realized that God created me EXACTLY how He wanted me to be, and that I am blessed to be alive today. The more I grow closer to God, the more I know how loved I am. This is awesome. Even if I am in jail, I am loved. He saved my life and has enlightened me on so many wonderful things. I am so grateful.

Part II

Re-Create Your Own Reality

Within you is the ability to change
your ideas about reality and about yourself,
to create a personal living experience
that is fulfilling to yourself and others.

Seth — Jane Roberts

4 Shadows of the Light

You have come as Light, to transform darkness,
to move ultimately into the brighter remembering
of the Oneness that you are.
—Emmanuel

Once upon a time in a far away land called *Past*, an infant was born. The male baby had wide-set blue eyes and a small patch of straight blond hair around the ears and back of the head giving him the appearance of an old wise man. And wise he was, for within him he possessed all the wisdom and knowledge of the ages. He was well aware of the gifts given him before he chose to visit *Past*. Even though he could not speak to name it, he understood these gifts were his link to All That Is.

Often during infancy he would become very still and listen to the inner rhythms instructing and guiding his awareness. When he was in communion with these gifts of Light, his eyes would become clear and glassy giving him an out-of-body appearance. To his parents' dismay, at these times it appeared as if he was in some sort of coma. Not understanding their son's self-contentment, when they found him in this *unaware* state they would rush over to pick him up and encourage a reaction from him. They felt he just needed more stimulation and therefore brought him a myriad of baby rattles, hanging mobiles, music boxes, and other assorted toys. They also made sure not to leave their baby alone for any length of time for fear he might not stay in touch with "reality."

Soon the infant boy grew into a healthy young child. He rarely took time during these years to receive the inner gifts of wisdom for there was much to experience and attend to outside his own self-awareness. The young lad had learned well indeed that to go within was not really accepted or appropriate behavior. Instead he followed his parents' teachings

to keep busy, go play with the others, and to be a "good boy."
He learned early that in the land of *Past* all children were
expected to work hard, not cry or display emotions, and to
grow up quickly to be like the adults who ran the homeland.

Little did the young boy realize that while he adapted to
life in *Past* he was losing the gifts given him before entering
the land that would ensure his happiness. Oh yes, he would
take a brief moment now and then to listen to the rhythms
and touch the Light, but these opportunities became less and
less frequent as he grew into young adulthood.

His teenage years were fast and furious. There were lessons to learn; drugs to explore; sexual fantasies to discover;
family members to care for and appease; and the never-
ending thoughts of escape with which to cope. As you can
well imagine, there certainly was no time left for our busy
adolescent to go within and sense the enlightened rhythms of
his gifts.

When the young man became an adult, he knew exactly
how he should talk; how he should "settle down and earn his
keep;" and, how he should respect his parents' wishes. He
learned well what his parents and the adults of *Past* had
taught him. He focused on his goals to live in the land of
Future like everyone else did, while constantly striving for
success, contentment and happiness. He accumulated all the
right "stuff"—a wife, house, children, job, automobiles and all
the other important possessions.

Even though the young man followed all the *rules*, he expressed an empty present existence while living in *Past*. He
sadly admits that the once cherished gifts of inner wisdom
are seldom remembered. Only on occasion does a glimpse of
insight or a "lifelike dream" challenge his attention. At these
times he takes a few treasured moments to reflect on his
younger days as a child, trying to recapture the innocence
and love of life he once possessed. But alas, the once clear
channel of All That Is has become a mere *shadow of the
Light.*

~~

It has been said that the universe is but a spark of the Divine Light and we are fragments of that spark. When we were babies we were in touch with our gifts of Light, letting them shine for all to see. We would accept life spontaneously with curiosity and an eager ready excitement. Running through the grass, playing with animals, flying kites, and swinging high in the air on a seesaw were just a few of the fun-filled afternoons we experienced. However as we grew into adulthood, we allowed our openness and innocence to become shrouded with "shoulds" until we became mere shadows of the Light within us.

In the captivating true story *Mister God, This is Anna* detailing a young girl's magic, the author writes that to some extent "...all children have a touch of magic about them—like some mysterious living lens, they seem to have the capacity to focus the Light into the darkest and gloomiest of places." We all possessed this magic as children—*we still do*. It is our spiritual heritage. Anna's story tells of her ability to transform any malady into a learning, growth experience just like magic. She used her ability to literally re-create her reality by staying in touch with and using her gifts of wisdom and inner Light.

Anna instructed that we all need to allow our own Light to "come outside" if we want to make progress. To allow ourselves the opportunity to again shine our Light for all to see, "Letting your soul, or whatever fancy name you like to give it, out of its cage and into the daylight is perhaps the hardest thing anyone can do." Anna knew we all had our own spiritual-Self protected deep within us. She referred to this phenomenon as "...a vast assortment of little Mister Gods inhabiting the middles of everything....bits of Mister God which had to be put together like some gigantic jigsaw puzzle." According to Anna, your true-Self is seated securely in your *middle* and is your link to the unified God/Goddess/All That Is.

Psychospirituality

It is becoming more apparent in circles of psychological thinking that the body, mind, and spirit are acutely interconnected. Research conducted within the psychoneuron-immuneology, parapsychological, psychospiritual, and trans-personal fields is resoundingly clear: We humans are not only visible physical matter but unseen intellect, intuition, and spiritual essence generating as a connected life force. This insight brings a broader acceptance of the role our spiritual nature plays in our life and allows for the opportunity to move beyond the so-called normal psychology of man/woman into the paranormal.

The ability to search inward, as well as, look outside ourselves to sense our correct or appropriate behavior and belief systems unites psychology and spirituality to form our psychospirituality. We are no longer bound by the dominance of our parents' beliefs, a pre-selected religious system, or even our own self-imposed psychological framework. We possess the freedom to explore and find our true-Self—to follow our own mores. We can cultivate a meaningful life purpose with this new sense of inner personal awareness. We can look beyond our ingrained structures of belief (psychology) and uncover our enlightened psychospiritual makeup.

Taking responsibility for our psychospiritual health begins with the awareness of who we are—what are our beliefs and how did we adopt them? Today's emerging holistic view has been paramount in establishing the self-responsibility concept. Holism implies wholeness, an acknowledgement and acceptance of the total being. The implications of holistic health include an awareness of one's intent to be an active participant and assume responsibility for one's wellness. In keeping with this intent, it becomes important to check all levels of well-being, including your transpersonal or spiritual-Self.

As you begin to unravel the "whys" of your psychology—how you became who you are—seek answers and direction from this "inward arc." In her book, *The Inward Arc*, psycho-therapist Frances Vaughan writes:

> Learning to pay attention to inner experience is an essential part of maintaining mental health. One gains autonomy and self-determination not just by being free from external constraints, but by con-

sciously choosing goals and values and learning how to direct attention. The mind can be trained to think in any number of ways.... We know that the mind can be re-programmed, but conditioned patterns of perception tend to persist in the absence of self-awareness and conscious intention to change.

When the conscious intent to change is summoned a multiplicity of reactions are initiated. Once the desire to change and begin the process of opening to the Light is established a domino effect occurs. Inward reflection coupled with self-responsibility support change and transformation.

The ascending steps leading to psychospiritual integration can only be tread upon with the *individual's response to choice*. The task of integrating one's past woundedness with aspirations of healing the present and future is challenging. Vaughan instructs, "Becoming whole means learning to accept all of ourselves and heal the splits between shadow and persona..." This may happen very slowly with each thought, each new awareness; or, it can happen in an instant. *Spiritual awareness is a process not a goal—the path and the destination are one in the same.*

PSYCHOSPIRITUAL INTEGRATION

TRANSORMATION

CHANGE

ACTION

INSIGHT/IDEAS

STIMULATION

AWARENESS

INWARD REFLECTION

These steps toward a healthy personal vision can awaken our spiritual nature directing us toward re-creating our own reality. "Vision depends on Light," writes Vaughan, "...whatever one fears to see, whatever one hides in darkness, becomes an impediment to vision. When inner vision is ignored, one is caught in illusions that constrict awareness. Inner vision is a gift that is always available, requiring only attention for recognition. The Light is ever-present, awaiting only our willingness to experience it."

Many proponents within the traditional psychology arena feel the inclusion of the spiritual aspect (transpersonal) within the therapeutic framework is counterproductive to psychotherapeutic practices. They believe that to deal with the spiritual dimensions of their clients would be a deterrent to the psychological issues at hand. I decline to agree. We are moving into a more holistic model of therapy, one where *all parts equal something greater than the whole*. With this approach, how can we omit one part? This synergistic approach to healing and recovery must encompass the total being— body, mind, *and* spirit. It is with this holistic synergy that we can begin to reflect our inner gifts of Light out into our world.

Transpersonal Guide

In any healing and recovery process there is an element of the transpersonal at work. Re-Creation Therapy™ and Hypnotherapy in general readily employ this transpersonal aspect. In my book *Beyond Words: A Lexicon of Metaphysical Thought*, I define transpersonal as "trans" meaning across, beyond, or to change completely; and "personal," pertaining to the person or personality. Transpersonal is thus defined as beyond the person, or to change and reach across the personal awareness and individual ego. This interpretation fosters the ability to grasp the total personhood (body, mind, and spiritual nature) reaching beyond our familiar level of ego awareness to a critical examination of behaviors, thoughts, and emotions which spur *conscious transformation.*

Conscious transformation (changes of which one is consciously aware) occurs when any of the following transpire: Changes in thinking regarding world views, personal beliefs and goals; changes in the feelings that surround motives, values, love, compassion, and support; and, changes in perception such as noting extrasensory perception (ESP) or awakened spiritual awareness. Changes such as these can be called *conscious self-transformation.* These conscious transformations are the building blocks of Re-Creation Therapy™.

The ultimate goal of transpersonal therapy is to guide one through the act of conscious self-transformation to a state of self-trust/acceptance/esteem/love. It directs one to develop the awareness of the *unfolding process*. A transpersonal approach may incorporate other types of therapies creating a broad perspective for healing and recovery. Jung's individuation process—to become a separate individual, "in-divisible" or whole—describes what transpersonal counseling ventures to accomplish.

Re-Creation Therapy™ summons the transpersonal-self to act as a *guide* to direct one to the appropriate experiences, memories, emotions, releasing of feelings, and ultimate re-creation of past woundedness and trauma to reveal the true-Self. It becomes evident as you begin working with the child within that this transpersonal guide is always available to show you which childhood memory to explore. You can trust your transpersonal guide to lead you to the appropriate experience and re-creation episode.

Our friend Anna was one of those rare beings who perpetually lived life from a transpersonal level. She explored not only her daily physical reality but also the levels of awareness which were beyond the senses of touch and sight, to the transpersonal level. Continually she would challenge herself and her beliefs with forward thinking questions and the assumption that anything could be re-created for "...difficulties and adversities were merely occasions for doing something."

Anna's short quest for knowledge expanded the author's values, beliefs, and curiosity for life. After knowing Anna just a few short years, Flynn relates:

> I shudder to think that for two years I was content to eat the stale bread of learning, when right under my nose Anna was busy baking new and crusty ideas. I suppose I thought that a loaf ought to look like a loaf. To me loaf and bread were synonymous, and at that time I hadn't the sense to see the difference. In some part of my mind I can still detect a feeling of shame, a flicker of anger, and a sense of wasted time, from that moment when I realized that the important word was bread—that bread could be

baked into an infinity of shapes. I hadn't the sense to
see that the shape of the loaf had nothing to do with
the food value of the bread. The shape was nothing
but a convenience. But my education had been too
much concerned with the shapes.

We all unconsciously allow our "bread of life" to be molded
into shapes of conformity to suit our family's needs, our culture's demands, and society's doctrines. As the above author
explains, it is not the "shape" of the loaf that is important but
the *bread* itself. Allowing ourselves to be molded into the
shapes our family and society dictated was a necessary step
in our process of maturation. We actually needed the guidance and instruction we received during childhood—it became our basic subsistence. However, all too often we find
much of our childhood conditioning is not appropriate in
adulthood.

As adults, it is time to reevaluate which kind of foundations and beliefs suit us in our present adult environment. It
is time to discover which values seem obsolete and exactly
where we stand on such issues as spirituality, politics, love
and compassion, social mores, and so forth. We no longer
need to cling to the ways of our parents' generation. We can
swing the window latches free and soar with our own inner
convictions.

This much *freedom of choice* may sound threatening at
first, for to alter or change beliefs one must establish *something better* with which to replace them. What will I believe in
when I make the choice to let go of old patterns, values, and
limitations? Who will I be when I decide to choose freedom
over restriction? How do I begin to choose?

To answer these and other questions which will surely
arise, look inward to your transpersonal guide. This inward
search may take years as you gain confidence in employing
self-direction, then again, it may take only a magical instant
to become more conscious of who you are *becoming*. Allow
yourself to touch the Light of the child within and dispel the
shadows.

Child Within Exercises

1. Now that you have touched your child within the next step is to connect with your transpersonal-self, or Higher Self. This aspect of your being will be a guide to help you meet and work with your inner child. Your transpersonal-self is all the positive Light within you. It represents the highest values and ideals you possess. Your transpersonal-self embodies your deepest felt dreams, your truest intuition, and your link with All That Is.

Take a few minutes to calm and relax your body and mind. Close your eyes, go within, and touch the center of your being with your mind's eye. If you were to make visible your transpersonal-self, what would it look like? Let your imagination relish this thought as you allow the vision of your transpersonal-self to form. When a clear picture has been established, feel the sensations of becoming your individual transpersonal-self. You may wish to write down in your Journal what attributes and qualities you found. Accept this truth—you *are* your transpersonal-self.

2. Another tool you can use to connect with your transpersonal-self is to put a large piece of drawing paper and an array of crayons on the floor in front of you. Sit comfortably with your back straight and begin to relax your body by taking in several deep breaths from your abdomen. Concentrate upon your breathing, in and out, in and out. Imagine the spirit of life entering your body with each inhalation. Feel yourself breathing in all the pure spirit that you desire for yourself.

Envision a color (or colors) as you inhale deep within all that is free, pure, and loving. See this color(s) flowing into your body, touching every part, every cell. *Feel* the color(s) throughout your entire being. Stay with this feeling of peace for a few moments then *slowly open your eyes*. Pick the color of crayon(s) which best match your envisioned transpersonal, spiritual color. Very slowly begin to draw the *feeling level* of your Higher Self. You may draw a few lines and swirls, or perhaps, a highly involved picture. Whatever you feel impelled to draw is okay. You will be drawing from an unconscious frame of mind—just let it flow through you.

Continue with this drawing until it feels complete. Put the crayons down and consciously look at your drawing. What color(s) did you choose? Is the color meaningful for you in some way? Do you find yourself drawn to the color(s) in some fashion? Can you feel your drawing and the color(s) in your body? In which part of your body do you feel the color(s) and your transpersonal-self? Allow yourself to expand upon this exercise by drawing other forms, pictures, or scribbles which you feel describe or explain this connection with your transpersonal-self. Let your inner spiritual feelings flow out onto the paper as you discover this inner guide.

Child Within Affirmations

My transpersonal-self is filled with Light.

I allow my spiritual nature to shine bright within me.

My transpersonal guide safely leads me to my childhood memories.

I open myself to explore my spiritual-Self.

I trust my transpersonal guide.

I keep my body, mind, and spirit in perfect balance.

Child Within Autohypnosis

In a quiet time and place, lie down on your back allowing yourself plenty of uninterrupted time to relax your body and mind. Focus your attention on the top of your head, find the warm energy there and bring it down into your body. You may sense a warm white light like a halo surrounding your head, bring this light down into the body. Feel this warm light relaxing the lines in your face and neck. Allow yourself to relax your shoulders, back and buttocks. Breathing in and out in a rhythmic fashion, relax your pelvis, legs, and feet. When you feel your body is completely relaxed, allow your mind to relax. Release any thoughts of anxiety, worries, or tension with each exhale. Exhale out all unwanted mind-clutter while releasing doubts and fears. You will touch your transpersonal-self as you begin to ease away all the tension.

Using the color(s) in Exercise #2 to focus on, concentrate on this color as you bring it down into your body starting from the top of your head. Sense it gently entering your face, neck, and shoulders. Feel the color enter your back, abdomen, legs, and down into your feet. *Feel* the intensity of this color as it envelopes every muscle, every cell. *Feel* its warmth and texture—hot or warm, soft, smooth. Can you taste this color? Does it have an odor? Use all of your senses to consume this color and feeling level until your entire body and mind is encased in the color(s) of your transpersonal-self.

Allow yourself to completely focus your attention on this inner guide wrapped in the magnificent color of your spirit. You may hear a whisper of a few words or an entire message from your guide. Listen carefully, the insight you receive may be a subtle sense of caring or a release of emotional energy. You may experience a tingling sensation in your body or a rush of excitement. Whatever you experience, it is right for you.

When you feel ready, open your eyes and write down in your Journal this experience of meeting your transpersonal guide and the direction or insight given you. You now can enlist the aid of your transpersonal guide to direct you to the appropriate childhood events and emotions as you continue on your journey of self-discovery.

Child Within Journal

The colors green and yellow streamed into my body, entering through my nostrils and flowing down the Rest of my body. It was an ebb and flow as I breathed in and out. I felt the colors tell me that I can make it through this jail expeirennce (sp?), peaceful and Relaxed. They were telling me that I am in a safe place and to just be patient and grateful. They were waRm and soft against my chilled skin. They formed a dragon-like creal creature as they exited my body. The creature was smiling and speaking to me directly to my face.

Child Within Journal

5 Mirror, Mirror on the Wall

> Only with the relinquishment of
> illusory self-concepts can the conditions
> for happiness be established.
> —Frances Vaughan

How many times have you stood before a mirror and asked yourself, "Who am I?" Interestingly, many people do not have an answer to this question. Lillian Rubin's research on self-concept as stated in her book *Women of a Certain Age: The Midlife Search for Self*, clearly shows most women cannot describe who they are as a person. When asked this simple question, the women interviewed went blank and offered statements like, "Maybe there just isn't much of a self there." It is a sad situation indeed when one looks into a mirror only to find a blank reflection.

Many of us respond to the question "Who am I?" with whatever labels we might have pasted on our foreheads which correspond to society's description of our duties within it. These societal labels are names and titles such as father, mother, secretary, teacher, executive, nurse, student, construction worker, and salesperson. This type of response is quite normal for we tend to believe we are what *others* perceive us to be. Examine your forehead closely, you might be surprised by the number of labels you have pasted there.

Many of the self-concept labels you have accepted originated in childhood and reside deep within your inner child. Some labels you could have accepted may include attitudinal beliefs such as do-gooder, stupid, airhead, bookworm, irresponsible, Mamma's boy, *just* average, and dumb blonde. Labels can also be physically descriptive like chubby, towhead, beaver, tomboy, shorty, homely, four-eyes, chunky, and bean-pole.

While dealing with my own self-image, I found several labels firmly glued to my forehead which were collected in childhood—two of these were "string-bean" (given to me by fellow first grade classmates) and "goof-butt" (a self-esteem destroyer dedicated by my father whenever I did not meet his expectations). There are no limits to the number of labels you may have adopted throughout childhood; however, now as an adult you can take the steps necessary to release them and capture a clear perspective of your true-Self.

In the book *Mister God, This is Anna*, we discover that in her search for self-understanding, Anna realized that we each accept false-selves by covering our true-Self with labels we have been exposed to in childhood. She explained that in childhood we shield ourselves with "bits of colored glass" hiding our view of ourselves and our world. Anna felt this was done unconsciously and that parents and peers also contributed to our "labeling process" to establish a form of control or manipulation.

The labels we accept while growing up become shields which cover our true-Self. In turn, these labels become the blockages which prevent us from attaining a positive self-image as adults. With labels like "not good enough," "bad boy," "perfect little girl," "good-for-nothing," and "dummy" we see ourselves through a stained-glass mirror. Anna said, "People got into the habit of slipping these bits of glass over their inward eye and seeing things according to the color and label of the glass." She felt our task in life was to tear away each bit of colored glass until our true-Self could be seen clearly.

In our society, labeling a person with a common put-down, for an event which was experienced, or from an out-sider's view point is common. In our society, we label those who drink alcohol "a lush" and "a drunk." Adults label children who need extra help learning in school "learning disabled" and children from divorced parents who come home to an empty house "latch-key kids." We label people who smoke "smokers" and those who do not smoke "non-smokers." We attach labels to ourselves which signify distaste and dissatisfaction with our lives such as "loser," "failure," "screw-up," "knuckle-head," and "dummy." What is important to remember is that each negative label you accepted in childhood, as well as, the ones you have accepted as an adult, are over-generalizations and can affect your self-concept and self-worth.

When we look at a mirror's reflection, we see what we *believe ourselves to be*. Self-concept simply means the *concept* we hold of ourselves. Our self-concept is derived from both our inner sensibilities (what we feel ourselves to be) and the outside influences we choose to accept as truth. This concept is the formulation of all the behaviors, attitudes, feelings, and other qualities we have established about who we are at this point in our life. We label ourselves by *accepting* (consciously and unconsciously) the above characteristics, as well as, other people's opinions of who they perceive us to be.

I once encountered this labeling process while giving a workshop. A gentleman in the audience was sharing his current recovery process from alcohol and proceeded to call himself "sick." He had derived from his recovery group members that he had a sickness and proceeded to conclude he was *sick*. Another participant asked to speak to this man and suggested to him, "Consider that you are not *sick* but perhaps were only *asleep and are just now awakening*." This statement lodged in my mind as an acceptable alternative to labeling oneself *sick* so I proceeded to encourage the recovering alcoholic to work with re-creating his self-image of being *sick* into one of *awakening spiritually*.

As therapist and author David Burns states in his book, *Feeling Good*, "Labeling yourself is not only self-defeating, it is irrational. Your *self* cannot be equated with any *one* thing you do. Your life is a complex and ever-changing flow of thoughts, emotions, and actions.... Would you think of yourself exclusively as an "eater" just because you eat, or a "breather" just because you breathe?" You are a diverse individual with many aspects which cannot be narrowed down to a mere handful of labels.

Self-image, self-esteem, and self-concept all relate to basically the same idea—who *you* think and believe yourself to be. Lazaris (a channeled friend) put it so well when he said:

> [Labels] are like steam on the bathroom mirror...
> they keep you from seeing yourself.

Through the blurred image your foggy shape becomes a scary monster, and you run rather then clean the mirror.

Do you hate yourself for being like a steamy mirror? Then why do you hate yourself for your mental fog?

You clean the mirror; you discover yourself.

Those adults who have a positive self-concept, healthy self-image, and high self-esteem are the ones who have worked through their childhood "labeling process" and continue to refuse "mislabeling" from others thus allowing a clean mirror reflection.

To re-create a healthier self-concept, learn to sort through the many labels with which you define yourself. This must be done very subjectively, only *you* can determine which labels are positive and which are negative. When a negative labeling attitude is found, replace it with a positive self-image affirmation. You have the ability to remove restrictive labels and re-create a positive, healthy self-image—*clean the mirror and discover yourself.* (Exercises in re-creating negative labels are included at the end of this Chapter.)

Should/Shouldn't Syndrome

Many clients I encounter in therapy are "should" orientated. Like the young man in the story at the beginning of Chapter Four, these people tend to use the word "should" or "shouldn't" repeatedly. I *should* be a better mother/father. I *should* take care of my parents. My wife *shouldn't* spend so much money on the kids. I *should* wash the dishes right after dinner. Burns calls this the "shouldy" approach to life, I call it the "Should/ Shouldn't Syndrome." It is easy to acquire this self-imposed syndrome but just as easy to eliminate it.

If you catch yourself speaking in "shoulds," stop immediately and replace the sentence with another. For example, instead of saying, "I shouldn't eat so much candy" replace your words with "I *choose* to eat less candy." Or, instead of commanding, "You should pay more attention to your kids" offer "I am sure your kids would appreciate your attention." Another suggestion to test yourself regarding the

Should/Shouldn't Syndrome is to actually mark down on paper each time you use the word should or shouldn't. In this way, you can discern quickly and accurately whether you have adopted this condemning and restrictive behavior. When you catch yourself saying either of the two words decide if you can replace it with could, would, can, wish to, or do not want to. If you can retrain yourself to use other words in place of should/shouldn't, you will obtain a greater sense of control and self-esteem.

One of my clients, Jill, came to me with a low self-concept and had acquired the Should/Shouldn't Syndrome. She was raised in a traditional family with much expectation surrounding the proper behavior for a young girl in the 1940s. Jill's parents are artistically oriented and established early in her life that she *should* be an artist, specifically a dancer. She went to dance schools but did not excel in her lessons. Though Jill's parents did not overtly show their disappointment, she felt she had hurt them deeply.

Jill felt like a "failure" because she did not accomplish what she felt she *should*. She sensed as a child that she *should* have been more like "Shirley Temple with a performing talent and cute with curly hair, not the straight dull hair I had." Therefore, she tried various other artistic endeavors such as singing lessons and the creative arts, always trying desperately to please her parents. However, with each new attempt, Jill did not complete the training. She stated, "I felt as though I was trying to become someone I was not just to please my parents." Consequently, Jill grew up with deep feelings of inadequacy and a poor self-image.

The labeling process in childhood, whether accepted from outside influences or self-imposed, can "make or break" our self-worth. Jill felt she had "let her parents down" by not becoming the creative, artistic child she knew they desired her to be. During her childhood, she kept this secret locked within trying desperately to win their love while at the same time trying to overcome her feelings of being a "failure."

When Jill excelled in the academic world, she finally began receiving support and recognition. This validation came mostly from her professors and peers—very little from her parents. As Jill began exploring her self-concept issues and her child within, she acknowledged the many successes she had attained throughout her life. While in hypnosis, she allowed her inner child to show her how she had buried feelings of worthlessness so deeply that she had been living her life from this point of reference. By employing the techniques of Re-Creation Therapy™, Jill was able to re-create the "failure" label which she had accepted in her childhood into one of success and achievement. She visualized her parents applauding her achievements and accepting *her* choices.

During her therapy, Jill also chose to confront her parents regarding her low self-esteem and how it related to her childhood conditioning. This confrontation can only be a decision made by the individual and may not be an appropriate avenue for others, however, Jill found this course of action most helpful. She sat her parents down in front of her and asked them to please listen without interruption. She proceeded to explain her feelings of being a "failure" and how she felt she had failed to please them all her life. After she finished, Jill's mother and father expressed genuine concern and that they were glad she was able to share her feelings with them. They reassured her that they did not feel she was unsuccessful in her life. The three had a long discussion and afterward hugged and felt closer than ever before.

The Should/Shouldn't Syndrome can also lead to classic victimhood. The person who feels they *should* do or have been such-and-such is a victim of their own belief system. Those with a chronic dose of "self-victimization" are forever stating their life's trials and trauma. If you find yourself telling strangers and acquaintances about how you were used, led-on, ripped-off, or otherwise victimized, you may recognize this syndrome in yourself. Self-victimization always leads to blocked awareness, non-creativity, and an overall "give-in/give-up" type of attitude.

Feelings of unworthiness eventually arise when you impose the tactics of the Should/Shouldn't Syndrome because you can never live-up to everyone's expectations. If you continually think you *should/shouldn't* complete, learn, achieve, become, or *be* a particular thing then you are being a victim to your belief that another's demands or desires are more important than your own. Victimhood is an easy trap. Just when you feel you are "pleasing" others like you were taught you *should* as a child, you begin losing you own sense of life purpose and self-worth. *Your* needs and goals go out the window the minute you allow self-victimization to enter your life.

In Wayne Dyer's best seller *Pulling Your Own Strings*, he states that you can even be a victim to yourself by allowing others to rule your emotions. Only *you* can decide whether you feel hurt, happy, angry, afraid, lonely, content, peaceful, or depressed. Do not allow another person to impose upon you what *they* believe you *should* be feeling. Other self-victimization traps include working in a job you are not happy in (or not having a job) because *that is what I chose to do when I was young*; or, living in the same town because *this is what my parents said would be best for me*; or, feeling yourself to be unworthy, unattractive, not creative, not intelligent, and so on, because *this is the self-image I have had since childhood.*

It is time to remember *who you are.* You are a unique (one of a kind) individual (whole by yourself) human being (rare intelligent species) with your own personal spiritual guidance. Dyer writes, "You are always a worthy, important human being, and there is never any reason to conduct yourself, or allow others to pull or push you, in any direction in which your basic merit as a human being is challenged." By be-friending yourself, being aware of the traps to self-victimization, and refusing to get caught in the Should/Shouldn't Syndrome, you can continue to develop a healthy self-concept. (Further details concerning self-victimization and victimhood are covered in the following Chapter.)

Spiritual Reflections

The topics of self-image and self-esteem have been in the forefront during the current surge of recovery therapies. Also, our government has gotten into the arena by establishing nation-wide task forces to deal with the decline of healthy self-image and self-esteem concepts in our youth population. In the state of California, a task force entitled *Toward a State of Esteem* presented its final report in January of 1990 only to find that their work barely scratched the surface of our long-awaited look at the devastating effects that a dwindling self-image can have on a child and subsequently their self-esteem as an adult.

The task force's official definition of a person with good self-esteem is: "Appreciating my own worth and importance and having the character to be accountable for myself and to act responsibly toward others." This is a workable definition which I would like to discuss in three parts. First, "appreciating my own worth and importance" involves the issues surrounding self-awareness and self-acceptance.

As stated earlier, self-awareness is the giant first step in healing and recovery. Looking into that mirror on the wall may be scary for it risks the possibility of discovering negative traits in yourself. Whatever you discover, see it clearly then instruct yourself to become aware of all the positive qualities you possess and acknowledge and appreciate them. True self-acceptance can come only after you have looked yourself straight in the mirror; gone through an emotional release process; exercised reprogramming of negative events and beliefs; employed forgiving; and finally, set realistic goals for the future. Self-acceptance and appreciation is the important second step to establishing self-esteem and a positive self-image.

Second, "having the character to be accountable to myself" states that you have developed a strength within yourself to be a responsible adult. Your decisions and actions are based on your understanding and awareness of the reality you are co-creating. Taking responsibility for your physical health, spiritual growth, and being accountable for your actions is the third step. And finally, "acting responsibly toward others" demonstrates a spiritual dynamic between the trust you have in yourself and the genuineness of your actions. Being able to respond to others; encourage independence of self and others; respecting the dignity of others; and fostering spiritual evolution becomes the fourth step in ensuring personal self-esteem.

The steps then to a healthy self-concept and self-esteem are:

1. Self-awareness

2. Self-acceptance and self-appreciation

3. Taking responsibility for your actions, and

4. Acting responsible toward others

These guidelines, and a desire to grow in this spiritual manner, invite a healthy self-image, as well as, a sense of spiritual growth perhaps not yet experienced. Author, doctor, spiritual seeker and teacher M. Scott Peck once stated that spiritual growth is the evolution of consciousness. He spoke of how over ninety percent of our actions are driven by our unconscious or subconscious mind and to be fully conscious of who we are we must bring our conscious and unconscious minds into synchronism.

Peck goes on to say that he feels so much of our Being-ness is *unconscious* because this is where we are connected to our God. We no longer need to search *outside* ourselves for God. We need not strive to become "one with God" because we already are. We no longer need to assume our evolutionary goal is to ultimately "unite" with God. Our true-Self *is* God. What then is our spiritual goal? The goal is to be more like God while we are conscious. In other words, after inner deliberation we can make *conscious* choices and decisions. *This* is as close to God as we can get.

Spiritual power is consciousness. It is the ability to make aware decisions, to manifest our desires, to live fully, to take care of ourselves, care for those in need and for our planet, and to recognize every day the miracles around us. *You* possess the spiritual power to achieve these goals. You can live from your true-Self while consciously accepting your part in the co-creation of your reality. Look *behind the mirror* to witness God through your own true-Self.

I offer this spiritual view point because I see many people who desire healing but do not feel comfortable with the way many "Twelve Step" programs deal with the spiritual nature. These programs ask their participants to acquiesce to something "outside" themselves, requiring them to give up their control (power) to a "Higher Power." Many of my clients have stated they could not relate to the loss of power they witnessed while in these groups. These clients state they need to feel "in control" to sustain their life and others feel they just want to keep what little sense of power they have managed to procure throughout a life filled with powerlessness. For these people to admit they have no control (power) regarding their addiction or situation is too great a risk.

To guide these clients toward healing, they were asked to begin acknowledging their own spiritual power by claiming their individual "power of choice" thus giving them the needed control to begin their recovery. They were directed to explore their feelings of control, power of choice, child within, repressed emotions, and their spiritual nature. Also, they were encouraged to attend various groups for support and nurturing. This course of action puts the responsibility back into the hands and hearts of the individual, not a group, not an unreachable Higher Power, and not family members. This is not to say the Twelve Step programs are not valuable. It has become quite evident over the years these groups possess the necessary tools and support to direct a great number of people through their recovery journey. However, there are alternative approaches which can be explored *within* the Twelve Step systems.

Behind the Mirror

Remember the children's story *The Little Engine That Could* about the little red train engine that didn't think it could climb the highest hill? This engine huffed and puffed unsuccessfully to make it to the top until one day it finally *believed* it could make it. This strong belief in itself gave the engine confidence and the repeating of the affirmation, "I think I can, I think I can, I think I can" brought it the success it desired. What was it that made this little engine keep trying? Confidence and Commitment.

Confidence comes with learning who we are *and* being okay with what we find. Confidence is an attitude—a frame of mind housed in self-acceptance. Self-confidence can only come from within. If we feel we do not live-up to our own (and others') expectations, we lose self-confidence. If we feel we have accomplished what we (and others) desired, we gain self-confidence.

While taking a break from writing the other day, I witnessed an extraordinary act of self-confidence. I was sitting on my back deck which overhangs an ocean inlet. When the tide is high the sea water rushes up underneath the deck completely swallowing the land below. I watched in awe as a raven-colored cat proudly tip-toed along the three-inch wide railing which wraps around several homes. It leisurely and expertly pranced around the entire decking and jumped down right in front of me as if to say, "Hi, I just thought I would demonstrate to you what *real* self-confidence looks like!"

Like that cat, as infants we possessed one hundred percent confidence in ourselves and our reality. However, all too soon we encounter humiliation, teasing, mistrust, name-calling, threats, and punishment which eats away at our very core of self-confidence and self-worth. I am sure you have witnessed (and perhaps experienced) a mother or father who chastised and humiliated their child while in a public place. During this type of punishment, the child becomes a shriveled mass of doubts and fears. Each one of these embarrassing experiences undermines the child's self-confidence and chips away percent by percent the total self-worth and confidence he or she possessed at birth.

Often times our lack of confidence is felt in a particular area. This lack of self-confidence could be centered around career goals, intimate relationships, productivity, sexual performance, creativity, physical appearance, public speaking, or intellect. Take a brief moment to zero in on what area in your life is contributing to a lack of confidence. Make a note listing these areas in your Journal and study the following questions:

When did I begin feeling *not confident* in this area?

What childhood events tricked me into believing I could not excel in this field?

What person(s) directed my beliefs surrounding this subject?

What actions have I taken *since* the above experiences to test myself in this arena?

What can I do *now* to challenge myself and my self-confidence in this area?

If you *believe* you can be successful at something, you have a far greater chance of succeeding than if you believe you cannot succeed. Challenge yourself to explore those areas where you feel limited or not worthy. Sitting idly encased in your beliefs of failure and low self-confidence will assure your continued acceptance of negative conditioning from childhood. Remember, belief precedes experience. If you believe you can do it, you can! Richard Bach put it so well in *Illusions* when he wrote, "Argue for your limitations and they're yours."

Commitment belongs to ourselves. When we think of the word "commitment" images of responsibility, limitation, duty, obligation, or something we *should* do springs into our minds. However, think back to that "little red engine that could"—it possessed commitment. It made a vow, a commitment, to put all its effort and all its confidence to a self-test. *That* is commitment, self-commitment, the kind of commitment which is dedicated to being the best you can be in all areas of your life. When you can make a commitment to yourself that you are ready to let go of your conditioned childhood beliefs and pain, you are well on your way to reclaiming the one hundred percent self-confidence issued you at birth.

Many adults today are hurting emotionally. The evidence lies all around us. One giant red flag is the millions of Americans who choose to grasp at reality only to clutch bottles of pills, glasses of alcohol, drug needles, junk food binges, or a prescription slip in their hand. Our need for stimulants, depressants, food, and/or mind altering drugs is beyond our

measurable realm. Why do we need these addictive sub-
stances and behaviors? America answers: To blot out the
reality of pain and the pain of reality.

Our perception of this painful reality originates in childhood, most likely from parents who also felt the same pain in
their childhood. Parents are our models whether they want to
be or not and with this role they are given a script from *their*
parents. We begin taking our acting cues from these parental
scripts and play a fictitious role filled with woundedness and
pain. These scripts include silence and denial; low self-
esteem and self-worth; competitiveness; greed; feelings of
rejection and abandonment; guilt and shame; and self-
victimization. Scripts such as these are handed down for
generations among families and most often are never up-
dated or edited to suit the current decade or the individual.
Therefore, this behavioral patterning of passing various roles
down from parent to child leads to dysfunctional family systems.

Research has proven that children of alcoholic parents
have a lower self-esteem than those who do not come from
homes where alcohol was abused. I believe the same results
would be revealed in all parent/child relationships where
there is any type of substance abuse, physical/emotional
abuse, or in families supporting a workaholic. This fact must
not be taken lightly. To heal our children, we must heal ourselves. To heal ourselves, we must not accept the "foggy,
scary" reflections we see in the mirror. It is time to expose
our illusionary roles and wipe off our blurred mirrors.

It is only human to care for those we love. Whether they
have an addiction to alcohol, drugs, food, or work does not
take away our desire for them to be happy or belay our love
for them. Janet Woititz has shown us how easy "the family
members get caught up in the consequences of the illness
and become emotionally ill themselves." In my own dysfunctional family, I was always looking to others for validation,
struggling with fears of rejection, seeking approval from my
father, stuffing my emotions, and feeling confused about my
own worthiness. These characteristics "within childhood" are
not looked upon as particularly abnormal, however, if carried

into adulthood these same personality traits are considered unstable, sometimes pathological.

Why is it that we allow our children to continue through-out their childhoods feeling "less than acceptable" then as soon as adulthood is deposited upon them at some undeter-minable age, we assume they should understand instinct-ively how to act and feel as a healthy, productive, respons-ible, independent adult? This is the type of mirroring behavior we must rethink and soon intercede if we are to heal ourselves and our children. We must look *behind the mirror* to witness God/Goddess/All That Is through our own true-Self's reflection.

Child Within Exercises

1. Find a full length mirror, stand in front of it. Look first at your feet—move your toes and get a sense of how your feet keep you balanced. Look at your lower legs and knees—study the large muscles, the skin texture, and the thickness of the upper thighs. Now focus on your abdomen, chest and shoulders. Slowly move your attention up to the neck and finally your head.

Allow a specific word or phrase to accompany the different parts of your body as you skim the mirror's image. These words may elicit either a positive or a negative response. Note which parts of your body evoke which types of response. When a negative response occurs, close your eyes and recall the time in your life when you began thinking of yourself in this fashion. Remember the feelings accompanying the experience. Did someone call you a "name?" Were you trying to be like someone else? What were the exact circumstances surrounding your belief in this label?

Once you have searched and explored the issues which established the acceptance of a negative label, close your eyes and go into a light autohypnosis to experience the events and emotions surrounding the self-labeling. Your transpersonal guide will lead you to your inner child allowing him/her to replay the script. Let the feelings flow....

Now, while still in an altered state of consciousness, re-create the negative circumstances with a positive outcome; replace the negative labeling with a healthy self-image. Continue re-creating each negative self-image label you find in the mirror until your true-Self is reflecting back to you.

2. In your Journal make a list of the labels you feel you have accepted for yourself. They may be some of the prior labels you have worked with in Exercise #1. Allow the list to be as long as possible. After you have listed as many labels as you can, take your pen and slowly go down each word until it automatically stops—*circle that word*. Continue down the list in this manner, circling those words where your pen stops. Trust your intuition to stop your pen where needed.

Go down the list of words a second time and write the circled words on a separate page. Focusing on each word, take a moment to sense with your transpersonal-self when you accepted the self-labeling condition. A particular experience or event may pop into your mind or perhaps a feeling or sensation of the word itself may enter your awareness. Stay with your feelings allowing yourself to explore the experience. Does this label feel positive or negative to you? How old were you when you pasted this label to your forehead? Were there certain people around you which influenced your accepting this label? If a negative label, do you understand why you accepted yourself in this limiting manner?

The negative labels may be blockages, or "bits of colored glass" you have not recognized until now. As in Exercise #1, close your eyes in a light autohypnosis and allow your transpersonal guide to take you back to the child within and the circumstances in which you decided you would accept the limiting negative label. Meet your inner child and let him/her explain what happened. When you feel you have grasped the meaning of the situation and understand why you took on the label, go back and re-create the events and their attached emotions the way you would have liked to experience them. With your child within, literally re-create the situation and surrounding feelings reprogramming your subconscious mind with positive praise and desirable attributes. Allow the "bits of colored glass" to break away displaying a crystal clear image.

3. The relationship you have with yourself is the most important relationship you have or will ever have in the future. This relationship is between you (the image you hold of yourself) and your true-Self. This intimate relationship is the foundation for your self-image. If your self-image is less than positive, you experience yourself, your relationships, and your reality in a "less than" frame of reference. Promoting a positive, balanced, harmonious relationship with yourself is the basic ingredient for personal spiritual growth.

Take a few minutes to turn your thoughts back to your childhood allowing memories to flow to you regarding the spiritual (religious) teachings and actions you experienced.

Who was your primary spiritual teacher? Were you required or forced to attend a regular type of religious gathering? Bring to your conscious mind the main values and beliefs instilled upon you as a child. Do you still feel obligated to enforce any of these? How did your spiritual up-bringing influence your current self-image?

Use this opportunity to study your personal spiritual evolution then take responsibility for what *you* believe. You may wish to investigate different spiritual communities or belief systems if you do not feel connected to any one in particular. The following poem titled "Inside Out" by Jed Diamond embodies our spiritual journey:

> I am taught what I am
> I live out what I am
> I explore what I am
> I cannot hide what I am
> I am just fine as I am
> I am as deep as Creation
> I am One with Creation
> I am a man/woman.
>   (Fifth Wave Press, 1983)

Child Within Affirmations

My self-image grows more positive each day.

I accept who I am.

I am a caring, successful person.

I choose to see my true-Self's reflection in the mirror.

Child Within Autohypnosis

Lie down on your back, close your eyes and begin to relax your body and mind. Breathe deeply filling and emptying your lungs completely. Feel the rise and fall of your chest as you breathe. Focus your attention only on your breathing, note how long it takes you to complete the cycle of inhalation and exhalation. Sense the clean air entering your lungs then surging through your body. Upon each exhale release the tension surrounding your chest, back, and abdomen. You may wish to "sigh" with your exhales in a total releasing manner. Allow your jaw and mouth to relax and begin to feel your mind drifting.

Still focusing on your chest, sense a glow of warmth and/or radiating light coming from this area. You can almost feel it circling, swirling within you. Take a moment to feel the presence within....

This warm glow may be the size of a pea or as large as a melon. Whatever the dimensions, this light begins to grow. Slowly it circles and spins within your chest. Slowly it grows becoming a brilliant light within you. As it grows and expands, you feel it encompassing your entire body and mind. You may sense that you are becoming softer, lighter, more solid, peaceful, or as if you were floating—*whatever* you experience is right for you.

Allow yourself to touch your true-Self. Stay close to this spiritual reflection—explore it, feel it, nurture it. *IT* is you—your true self-image, free of limiting labels and restricting beliefs. You have experienced that part of yourself which is free of limitation, free of victimization, free from condemning labels. Keep this image with you the next time you look into the mirror on the wall.

Child Within Journal

Child Within Journal

6   From Victim to Victory

> "It is the bliss of childhood
> that we are being warped most
> when we know it the least."
> —William Gaddis

Emma grew up in the Midwest in a family struggling against poverty. The youngest of four children, Emma was bounced back and forth between brothers and sisters who fought with and teased her. Her father was an alcoholic who abused his authority over the family with more than threats and her mother was a typical overprotective nurturing codependent wife.

When Emma was fourteen years old she dated a boy several years older and became pregnant. Hoping he would marry her, she decided to continue the pregnancy; however, after her son was born, Emma's boyfriend claimed he was not the father of her child. She brought child support charges against him in court only to lose her case for unclear reasons except that she could not "prove" she had intercourse only with her boyfriend during the time she had conceived.

Emma continued to live with her parents while raising her son, not dating or going out socially. She fed her feelings of anger, guilt, and shame by preventing herself from living a normal adolescence. She stayed at home consuming endless amounts of coffee and cigarettes stimulating and nurturing a chronic depression. When Emma finally ventured out into the social world she was a young adult and met her future husband in a local bar. They married soon after they met and had two children.

Now tied to her own alcoholic, Emma continued her suffering which encouraged her familiar life script of victimhood. Always ready to tell of her pain and suffering, her self-victimization flourished. As the years passed, Emma grew tired, weak, and old by the time she was thirty-five. It was at this point she started realizing all her projections of a painful life were exactly what she had produced. She expressed a desire to change her self-image and tried to break free from her strangling relationship but her efforts were again swayed. She felt she could not fight any longer. At forty she was diagnosed with massive cancer throughout her body. A victim, Emma died at age forty-two.

Emma's story is perhaps a sad tale to which you may respond with questions like, "How could she let herself be so abused and used all her life?" or "Why didn't she pull herself out of her self-suffering rut and try to turn her life around sooner?" It is far easier to sit outside someone's life and ask "why" than it is to actually experience it. In Emma's reality, she felt "good" about her choices and that she did "the best she could" to make her life work. She, in fact, thought she was honoring her strong beliefs about life and suffering which were handed-down to her by her mother. Emma lived out her short life knowing she was fully supported and loved by her mother, this became her most important reward.

In the previous Chapter, the concept of playing out scripts in our lives was discussed. Self-victimization or victimhood is just one of the subconscious scripts we can continue to role-play in our adult life when we have been a victim as a child. A victim is "a person who has been cheated, fooled, injured, or killed." *Victimhood is that state of mind when one feels at the mercy of their reality and the undetermined length of time in which one "sustains" his or her feelings of self-victimization.* After reading Emma's story it becomes easy to understand how we can slip into a victim role or script without being aware of it. We can play out the role of victimhood while at the same time negating our true desires and miss many opportunities for change and growth.

We have all experienced the feelings of being a victim in our childhood in one way or another, even if only from our cultural heritage or society at large. Childhood experiences of being reprimanded, teased, laughed at, and bullied all carry the ingredients of potential victimhood. We learn at an early age how to "sulk" and of the woundedness associated with being a victim. However, it is important to get in touch with how we treat these feelings surrounding our victimization or we may find ourselves clinging to our suffering well into adulthood, perhaps even continuing the pain of self-victimization throughout our life as did Emma.

The Triggered Victim

Are you living out a life of roles and scripts which were handed-down by your parents? Can you find similarities between your choices in life and the choices taken by either or both of your parents? What were your parents exhibiting in their life at the same age you are today? Have you subjugated your true-Self for love and approval from your parents? If so, in what ways? (Write your answers down in your Journal.)

These are the questions to ask to distinguish if your choices in life have been based on your desires as an adult or if they stem from your inner child's desire to be accepted by your parents. By answering these questions and others, you may discover many of your scripts were initiated out of love and loyalty to your parents. (In his book *Pulling Your Own Strings*, Wayne Dyer has several self-tests on self-victimization and victimhood. I refer you to these tests if you have questions as to whether you have been a victim or are continuing a victimhood script.)

Self-victimization can be encouraged by well-meaning relatives and friends. Emma's mother would be the first to acknowledge just how "hard and painful" a life her daughter underwent. She was the typical self-sacrificing mother who would bend over backward to help her children. She encouraged Emma's victimhood by supporting the premise of how hard and painful life is for a woman. She gave Emma permission to rightfully feel used and helpless by allowing and encouraging her role of subjugation. This is an example of a handed-down life patterning script which can literally feed one's convictions of being a "victim of circumstance."

An even closer look reveals that Emma's decision-making skills and personal power were never encouraged as a child. The man of the house, her father, had the authority and power of decision-making within the family system. Next in authority were the two older brothers leaving the women on the low end of the scales. Emma learned early in life that she was to be like her mother, a victim in a male dominated environment. Many other factors surrounding Emma's family history contributed to her feelings of low self-worth and self-victimization and cannot be fully explored in this context; however, you may be able to relate some of your own self-victimization patterns by comparing yourself with Emma's inability to recognize her life-long script of victimhood.

In my own dysfunctional family system with an alcoholic father, my two sisters and myself were victims of abuse. Experiences of any kind of abuse in childhood can easily spur feelings of rage, anger, guilt, shame, unworthiness, low self-esteem, depression, and much woundedness. One does not need to experience violent abuse as a child to feel the pain of being a victim. If you have been a victim of any abuse whether physical, emotional, psychological, or spiritual, you begin relating to others and yourself in a new way. Many times your entire day is focused on when or if you will be a victim once again.

This patterning or scripting can remain ingrained in the subconscious mind well into adulthood. These roles may be hidden from your conscious awareness only to slip out now and then when you are around those who encourage the behavior. To demonstrate how another individual can trigger an old childhood pattern or behavior, let me tell you about an incident which happened to me as a child and how I buried my emotional reactions to it for several years.

My father, as lovable as he sometimes could be, often demonstrated many of his own childhood patterns. One of these annoying behaviors was to become an "untouchable" when he did not get his way or was angered by another person. He would become silent and not talk to the person with whom he was upset or displeased. I remember only too well this "silent treatment." Once when I was about nine years old, I decided to cut my long hair very short, trying to copy the look of one of the prettiest girls in school. I knew Daddy liked my hair long but I was not prepared for the strong reaction this elicited from him when he came home to find my hair short.

Daddy told me he did not like my new haircut at all then proceeded to not speak *one word* to me for two entire weeks. Even today I do not understand why cutting my hair triggered such a painful reaction from him. At the time, I remember feeling very bad and only wanted him to forgive me. At nine years old, little did I realize I was a victim of the abusive treatment of "outcasting" me from his reality. This untouchable treatment, and the self-blaming reaction it triggered in me, became a problem in adult life when my husband began using this same behavior when he did not want to share his feelings with me.

When my husband became an "untouchable" it would trigger my child within and I would find myself feeling that familiar victim role again. However, now that I have acknowledged, released, and re-created that very upsetting event with my father over cutting my hair, I can quickly recognize when a person tries to use the *silent treatment* to shut me out or make me feel guilty. When this happens, I do not take the victim-stance any longer. I instead help them realize how their own inner child has been triggered into not talking and sharing.

I also have learned how to listen to my child within and be assertive enough to speak up and talk about my feelings. After sharing with my husband about my childhood experience with my father's use of the silent treatment, he understood how his silence and emotional withdrawal triggered my old victim role. Subsequently, he has worked diligently to re-create his own behavior of childhood patterning of not sharing his feelings like his family had subconsciously taught him. He began to realize much of his own self-victimization patterns and why he retreats into the "untouchable" mode. Thankfully, we each have managed (most of the time) to arrest triggering each other's inner child feelings of victimhood.

Family Type–Casting

We tend to create similar situations in our lives until we become aware that the same experiences keep "happening to us." When you recognize a particular negative circumstance seems to repeat itself over and over, or a certain type of person reenters your life several times to your dismay, take a hard look into your childhood and search for the pattern or script which may be embedded in your subconscious mind which invites the same unwanted experiences into your life.

One obvious role we play in our childhood which can display itself repeatedly throughout adulthood is our location in the line-up of siblings and the expected script it bestows. A significant portion of the roles we assume as an adult are based on what was encouraged or discouraged in our childhood according to our position in the family system. If one of the youngest of the family as in Emma's case, you may tend to feel "the world *owes* you and nothing is your fault." Living in a family system as one of the youngest children can have its benefits, however, in the long run many times one is left with feelings of "always being taken care of" therefore not needing to strive for your best.

My younger sister, the baby of the family, was labeled "cute and artsy" which provided her with the script of becoming the sister with "so much artistic talent." Yet at the same time, this label silently implied to her that she was not as intelligent as her sisters. This label stayed with her through many adult years. She kept peace and received love in the family system by accepting her role as an artist and to not expect to be seen as a serious educational student. She began working with her child within and chose to break the bonds of being type-cast as the "artistic baby" of the family. To do this she chose to continue her education and allowed herself to follow her true-Self's desire to become a writer, as well as, a successful bronze sculptress.

Many times when one challenges the casting of the family scripting and ventures outside the accepted boundaries, it disrupts the accepted family system. When this occurs, family members do not know how to relate to the child/adult's new found identity. This is why it is so difficult to move forward by trusting our own inner feelings of "who and what we want to be when we grow up."

We continue to live in our programmed scripts, not venturing beyond the boundaries established so clearly by our family system, we subconsciously fear that to challenge our role in the family unit would consequently result in our losing their love. We can become so embedded in our childhood slotted-roles that many of us live out our adult years content to stay the oldest, smartest, funniest, prettiest, dumbest, youngest, weakest, ugliest, strongest, or fattest child in the family to prove that we can be just what they all thought we would be!

If you find yourself relating to this concept of being slotted into a particular type of role by your family, it is now possible to re-create these influences. What your parents and siblings said and did to you as a child may have had a substantial effect on how you perceive yourself today. However, you can alter how you were regarded by your parents and others by re-creating (while in light autohypnosis) your beliefs into a mindset of what you would have wanted them to say about you.

As an example, you may have enjoyed playing the piano or painting as a child but this was discouraged by your parents. Instead, you were encouraged to enter competitive sports. As an adult, you may still view yourself as athletic but not artistic or creative. We have all heard of the person who developed a second career later in their life and became very successful. It is as if the desire and talent had been there all along just waiting to be discovered. This self-discovery can begin any time you choose. You can unlock these hidden talents and desires rather than continue to cheat yourself by believing there are limits to your abilities. In a gentle autohypnosis, search your subconscious mind for a time in your childhood in which you were happy doing, or attempting to do, something you enjoyed. Feel the energy of this action as you begin to dance, play the flute, paint, jump the high-jump, throw the ball, or write the poem just like you wanted to when you were a little boy or girl. This exercise may bring back one of your hidden talents long forgotten and discarded. Now you can follow through with your dream. Let yourself explore the new possibilities of choice in your life. *Become who you know yourself to be.*

A friend once told me that I work with people who have come to an "intersection in their lives." I like this analogy and have repeated it to clients when they tell me they need to make a decision in their life. If you have read this far, you most likely are one of those people who wish to move past being a "victim of circumstance" and begin creating a new way of being. The choice-point to move in a new direction, to look at the intersections of your life, and to choose which path to take is a giant leap forward. As we choose to face our fears and self-doubts, we begin to see these intersections as mere skid-marks along our journey to healing and wholeness.

Victims No More

If you are a victim of childhood abuse as I and my sisters were, you are a "survivor." Much has been written about child abuse and the survivors of it. This is only the beginning of the battle to enlighten those who are unaware while supporting those who are choosing to inspire changes. Statistics show us that our nation ranks high in the incidence of child abuse. This sad fact coupled with our nation's heavy addiction to alcohol, medication, and drug use clearly points to the imperative need for an in-depth look at our societal profile. Have we as a nation matured at all regarding our assumptions, education, or actions toward halting the abusive behavior imposed upon our children? Sadly, I say very little.

When I was counseling young women in a women's medical clinic in the late 1970s, I became familiar with the "story" of our physically, emotionally, and spiritually abused female population. For five intensive years, I sat and listened to literally thousands of young women (twelve years old being the youngest) who had "accidentally" gotten pregnant or were terrified that they had. They shared their stories of incest, date rape, and psychological abuse. These girls had grown up in the "enlightened" decades of the 1960s and 1970s but were *not* enlightened about their own bodies or their rights to choose what to do with them.

Sexual abuse, whether physical or emotional, is a national outcry. We have witnessed its effects on ourselves and our children but still the constraints of society rule that to educate our young boys and girls in the areas of sexuality is taboo. Many of you reading this book grew up as I did in the *Donna Reed*, *My Three Sons*, and *Ozzie & Harriet* TV family era. Growing up in the 1950s, I thought sex and my body were topics not to be discussed with my parents and received "double-bind messages" throughout childhood regarding my sexuality.

This withholding of necessary information is legitimate *suppressed sex education* abuse. If we are not given accurate instruction and knowledge about our own bodies as a child, how can we be expected to make rational, intelligent decisions when we are faced with the decisions of our sexuality? Decisions during childhood and/or young adulthood involving sexuality, including self-sex (masturbation) can be made with clear personal choice *if* we have the benefit of honest sex education plus the opportunity to discuss our personal sexual values and feelings with a caring parent or guardian.

The dilemma of sex education, when to begin it and by whom, only becomes "talk" when there is evidence of incest or other sexual abuse in one's childhood. Many times the "double-bind messages" a child receives from abusive experiences and his or her own natural sexual feelings are frightening and confusing. When I was about four years old a boy the same age and I wanted to play a joke on my older sister. We had a playhouse situated in the far backyard which doubled as a tool shed. This little boy and myself told my older sister to come watch a play we were putting on just for her and called her into the playhouse. The boy and I had previously agreed that we would pull down our pants right at the moment my sister walked in, to surprise her. Instead, my father walked in. I was briskly grabbed by the arm screaming and taken into the house for a good paddle on a bare bottom.

Before, during, or after the spanking I received from my father, no one talked to me about what I had done. I was left with my own small child mind to try and figure-out why what I had done was so terrible to evoke such a response from my father. All this took place at about the same time my father had begun asking me to touch his genitals. If there was ever a "double-bind message" about sex, this was it! I learned it was okay to discover a male's body with my father but not on my own with a little boy my own age. The following few intimate episodes with my father, coupled with the lack of sex education I received, created much confusion and a great deal of ambivalence surrounding my own maturing sexuality.

Double-bind messages surrounding sexuality are also given by our society during the teenage years. When a son is allowed to go out on dates with a "pat on the back" and a "wink of an eye" but a daughter before leaving the house for a date is scrutinized and told to come "straight home" (implying something other than watching a movie must not happen), it is clear that we still live in a society with double-bind messages. Most of the young women I counseled at the clinic were so misinformed about their own bodies, and sexuality in general, that I found myself identifying with their *suppressed sex education* abuse which was still being enforced many years after I experienced it! If we do not provide adequate sex education for our children, our society will surely continue its inclination toward even greater numbers of abuse.

As survivors ourselves, we must take the necessary action to educate, enlighten, and share our personal stories to curb what has become a national epidemic. When statistics show figures that one in four women and one in eight men have been sexually abused as a child, it is time to come forward and be counted. Now is the time to explore our past childhood conditioning and experiences. Today is the day to set ourselves free from self-limitations and constricting emotions from being a victim of childhood abuse, whether physical, psychological, emotional, or spiritual.

Acknowledge to yourself if you have been living your life in the victimhood mode because of past childhood trauma. As an adult you have the power to control and direct your life and release this negating role. Let us take each other's hands in confidence and begin the healing of our past abuse. Let us be "victims no more" by using our own inner power. With this re-creation exercise turn your past victimization into your survival strength. Right now, read the next paragraph completely, then close your eyes and instruct yourself to re-create your victimhood.

> Quietly use relaxation as instructed earlier to allow yourself to feel safe and protected. You are a child again. Feel your true-Self all around you, protecting you. Your little body or mind has been abused. You are confused. There may be emotions of anger, pain, guilt, shame, and much confusion. You may not be able to put into words exactly what you are experiencing but you know you feel bad. Now, release these feelings by allowing yourself to cry, scream, or pound a pillow, whatever feels right for you in this situation. When you feel you have released the emotions surrounding this experience, re-create a different scene. Re-create a play in your mind in which you are enjoying the person with you. You feel your little child strong and healthy in body and mind. You can say or ask anything you wish of this person with you and they respond in love and caring answers. Your child within is happy and filled with love for him/herself and others.

Over the years I have re-created my childhood experience in the playhouse many times. It became easier and easier to envision my father sitting down right there beside that little boy and me. He talked openly about our bodies and why it is not appropriate to display them to others. He would tell me about how wonderful our bodies are and that we should cherish and take care of them. He would tell me my body is private and belongs only to me. He would ask me if I had questions about my body or if I wanted to talk to my mother. He literally became the father I had wanted him to be *at that moment in time.*

We have all been victims in childhood. The important point to remember and take action upon is how, as adults, we have the tools and the personal power to choose to stop being victimized by others or society. Let us stand tall and proclaim we will be "victims no more" nor allow our children

al ourselves and let go of our own victimhood,
ing society that we will not tolerate the abuse
nt of our children any longer.

Child Within Exercises

1. In this chapter you were introduced to the concept of being "slotted" into a role in your family system. Study your role as the eldest, one of the middle children, or the "baby" position. Or, perhaps you were an "only child," in which case you might be playing many of the roles discussed. Think back on the type-casting placed on you by your family and write in your Journal the roles you feel you needed to play in order to receive love and acceptance by your family members.

These life scripts are ingrained very early in childhood and may be difficult to recognize. Your parents have determined much of what you feel about yourself by placing you into a slot or role which is the way they perceived you to be while growing up. Even if you believe you have changed your slotted-role from childhood, check again, you may find that role just changed its makeup to assume a different part within your adult play.

- Were you the "scapegoat" of the family? Are you still receiving the anger and pain of others in your present life as an adult?
- Were you the oldest child of a large family who was "always responsible and took charge?" Are you today the main caretaker of your own family always making sure everyone is doing what they are suppose to?
- Or, were you one of the silent middle children who never felt approved of or recognized for your own individual talents? Are you still the adult who silently blends-in at home and/or work only to be left out of major activities and important decisions?

These are only a few of the ways being type-cast or slotted by your family can follow you into adulthood. To summon your true identity and release your predisposed family roles, write in your Journal all your creative, fun, intelligent, athletic, strong, sensual, funny, curious, and loveable aspects residing "inside" of you at this very minute. Check your inner and thoughts. Write down the things you vere either told you could not accomplish or eptable by your family. You may just find a new way of perceiving yourself that has long in your child within.

2. Do you feel that you were a victim of "suppressed sex education abuse" while growing up? If so, you have the opportunity to rectify your lack of sexual information as a child by using autohypnosis to re-create this deficit. Whether you received the extreme "double-bind messages" regarding sexual behavior as I did as a child or just felt your lack of sex education caused much confusion about your sexual identity, you can give your child within or young adolescent the correct, healthy sexual knowledge you desired when growing up.

Matters of sexuality are delicate topics to discuss with a child/adolescent and require sensitivity, patience, clarity, and rational understanding. Many of us as children did not receive this kind of support and sharing regarding our sexual questions. Take a moment now to close your eyes, assume a light autohypnosis and re-create a time in your childhood when you would have liked your questions about your body and your sexuality to be explained. Envision whomever you choose to answer all your questions thoroughly and with care—this can be your parents, sister, brother, guardian, or grandparent.

You may also wish to talk about sex to your child within as the adult you are today. To do this, meet with your child within in a visualization or write to him/her in your Journal. Choose an appropriate child within age depending upon the topic you wish to discuss. Sit down together to answer questions and explore your inner child's lively curiosity. You may wish to re-create this scene several times at different age levels to fully bring yourself to a feeling of complete acceptance with your sex education as a child and young adult.

3. Do you automatically become a victim when you feel anger directed at you? Do you always blame others for your circumstances in life? When you argue a point with another person, do you hear yourself using childish language to get

your way? If you lose an argument, do you pout and/or use old childhood behaviors to make the other person feel guilty? Do you feel like a victim when you do not get your own way?

Answer the above questions in your Journal honestly. If you find that you do indeed feel a familiar link to victimhood by answering "yes" to any of them, you can take this opportunity to re-create your victimhood into victory. Whatever made you feel like a victim as a child influences the same reaction in you today. We strive for love and affection from our family (especially our parents) all our lives. By continuing your victimhood, your inner child is still trying to please his or her parents.

We attempt to honor our parents and family by trying to play the roles that they mentally slotted us into as a child. The depth of these silent agreements can show up in many areas of our life including how we employ these same victim games with our own children, thereby handing them down from generation to generation. To secure victory over your victimhood be honest with yourself about how you play the role of victim.

In your Journal write "an unmailed letter" to your family explaining you no longer wish to comply with the slotted roles given you as a child. Tell each family member you are re-creating your family roles and are learning to accept your true creative talents and individual attributes. Tell them you are firm about your conviction to change your victim role and your desire to leave it in the past. You may wish to begin the letter by again writing with your non-dominate hand which will bring you closer to hearing the words of your child within. The sooner you understand why you have chosen victimhood as a means of patterning behavior, the sooner you can let go of it and move forward toward your own strength and rightful place as a powerful, successful adult.

Child Within Affirmations

I willingly give up being a victim of circumstance.

My child within guides me to my strong, healthy Self.

My family loves me even though I have decided to be/do what I choose.

I choose victory over victimhood.

Child Within Autohypnosis

In a quiet place, lie down on your back and relax your body. To help you completely relax, take several deep breaths exhaling out of your mouth any tension or stress. Upon each exhalation *feel* your muscles go limp and soft. In your mind's eye go to each body part (legs, arms, back, neck, etc.) and tell it to let go and relax. Each time you close your eyes to relax your mind opens to insight and suggestion. Your body relaxes with each exhale. Reassure yourself that your child within will choose a childhood event during this autohypnosis to re-create which will enlighten and heal your feelings of victimhood.

Now that you are completely at ease and relaxed, begin counting downward in your mind very slowly from your present age. As you descend downward with each age, envision yourself briefly in this time period. Continue slowly.... 43, 42, 41, 40, 39.... 22, 21, 20, 19. With each number sense yourself at that age, become younger and younger until your inner guidance instructs you to stop.

At whatever age you arrive in your mind's eye, become familiar with the child you once were at this age. Notice what is happening. Are there others with you? What kind of clothes are you wearing? Allow the images to flow naturally following them like a motion picture before your eyes. You as an adult can observe the events and circumstances as an outsider as your child within re-experiences the emotions attached to this event. Follow this brief episode of your past allowing yourself to understand how you felt as a victim. If you have a strong emotion surrounding this experience, now is the time to express it. Allow yourself to cry, yell, or pound a pillow or two.

After you feel completed with releasing your emotions, easily and effortlessly take a moment to adjust your senses and look again at the event which caused you so much woundedness. Take a few minutes to *re-create this scene*. Allow your child within to direct you to what you would have wanted to have happened on this day in his/her life. Sense the people in this event the way you as a child would have

liked them to be—taking care to have them talk to you, hold
you, or instruct you lovingly. You can successfully accomplish anything in your autohypnosis which feels right for you
and your child within at this moment.

When you have thoroughly completed re-creating this
event, gently allow yourself to awaken from the autohypnosis
trance staying relaxed with your eyes closed. You have successfully re-created a traumatic event in your life with the
guidance of your child within. Tell him/her how grateful you
are for the guidance and direction. Tell him/her you love
them. Now, slowly count yourself back up to your present
adult age. In your awareness of each age, sense it clearly
with a *new enlightened view of who you are becoming*. Allow
memory of this re-creation to enter the workshop of your
mind and fill it with **victory**.

Child Within Journal

Child Within Journal

Part III

Adult Child
Games

One must enter the theater of the subconscious
like a safecracker and break the child's code
that is spoken there.

—Ariel Orr Jordan

7 Codependency Take Two

> We heal by remembering, literally bringing back
> into the wholeness of our being
> that which we have lost by hiding it
> from ourselves.
> —Joan Borysenko

When my mother first started reading my initial manuscript for this book, she looked up at me and asked, "What do you mean in the Introduction by my being a codependent?" My mother, being an intelligent and well read person, caught me by surprise with her genuine lack of knowledge about the meaning of codependence. I found myself somewhat embarrassed about the necessity to explain to my mother what for most of my life I saw her doing with hers.

I realized I had few words to describe to her just what being codependent meant. I tried using phases such as, "too dependent on her husband," "not caring enough about herself," and "restricting her own life because of her husband's demands." These broken sentences came easily but still did not touch on the real feelings I associated with the term codependent. Finally, I looked at her and said softly, "Mom, it just means that you cared so much for Daddy that somewhere along the way you lost *yourself.*" She understood and accepting this definition lowered her head to continue reading.

The surge of interest in the recovery field has led us to this nebulous issue of "codependence." Some leading experts claim we all have a codependent-self, a side of us which withdraws, avoids, and denies ourselves. Others maintain codependence is a disease or illness which requires psychological methodologies and sometimes medical intervention. To assume an illness one must demonstrate a physiological, psychological, or emotional dysfunction; therefore, to label one who nurtures and cares deeply for others a codependent

under this rationale would commit 99% of our female population to pathology! Only when one is nurturing others *to the
exclusion of themselves* can the ill effects of codependency be
labeled unhealthy.

One of the latest definitions of what constitutes a codependent personality comes from a group of professionals who
spent several hours of deliberation to confirm: "Codependency is a pattern of painful dependency on compulsive behaviors and on approval from others in an attempt to find
safety, self-worth and identity. Recovery is possible." This is a
good working definition, however, *codependency is an individual game played by two.* We must not forget it takes two
to form a codependent relationship.

A codependent personality does not occur unless there is
another person whose love and approval is so desired it becomes more important than our own. When this happens,
the person is "dependent" upon that other person to provide
all their love, affection, approval, and self-worth. In actuality,
they become the "co-operative dependent" just to receive the
love and approval they desire. They become codependent—
they become dependent themselves by cooperating with the
demands of others. This cycle of behavior is demonstrated
clearly in the case of those addicted to alcohol, drugs, work,
or most any kind of substance or behavior and are also in a
relationship. One partner is "dependent" on an abusive substance or behavior and the other becomes the "co" by their
mere collaboration. We must take care in not placing too
much emphasis on the codependent when it is the *addictive
behavior* of the loved one which is the primary issue.

I hear the term codependent being brought up in therapy
sessions more and more frequently without any real understanding of its meaning. Men and women are calling themselves a codependent, but at the same time cannot identify
the behavior which states they are in fact acting co-
dependently. To help identify if you are displaying codependent behavior, read down the following list of questions, feelings, and behaviors. Write a checkmark next to those
questions which pertain to you:

- □ Are you in a relationship with someone who you feel has an addiction to a substance or behavior, or both?

- □ Did you have a parent who was addicted to a substance or behavior, or both?

- □ Do you receive greater than 75% of your sense of value, self-worth, and/or approval from others?

- □ Do you, more than not, give up your power in decision-making to others?

- □ Do you turn your head in silence when your partner uses undesirable language or displays unacceptable behavior toward others?

- □ Do you "give-in" to the sexual desires of others without consciously considering your own?

- □ Do you feel stuck in a relationship which seems unbalanced in its giving and receiving of love and affection?

- □ Do you often use phases such as, "I don't care, whatever you think (or want to do)" and "Me too!" repeatedly?

- □ During disagreements with your partner, are you always the one who gives in?

- □ Do you use subtle manipulation tactics to try to fulfill your needs or get your own way?

(If you have marked "yes" to more than four questions above, you might entertain the idea that you have developed codependent tendencies.)

Many of you can identify with these types of questions only to ask, "What can I do about it?" One avenue to explore is when and where you first remember giving up your own inner power to another. Most likely this occurred as a child. Not yet able to understand how to draw on our own strength and sense of power, we learn early as children how to evoke a positive (or less than negative) response from our parents. We "try hard" to be the good little girl or boy that our parents want us to be. Not having the ability to fully nurture ourselves, we turn to our parents for caring and acceptance which sets the stage for this same kind of stratagem to receive approval and nurturing in our adult life.

If our efforts to receive love and approval are positively met by our actions of selflessness as a child, we continue this behavior unconsciously. We continue looking beyond our own sense of power for the nurturing we so desperately needed as a child and still require as an adult. This subconscious behavior to please others at the expense of our own desires is what codependency is all about. By going back in your memory to one of the first times you felt powerless by giving-in to a parent, guardian, or other family member you can unravel where your codependency began.

To assist you in this search, look at the list of questions once again. Note the ones marked "yes" and choose one or two of these behaviors which you feel are the most important links to your codependency. Each of these behaviors could initiate a memory of your childhood in which you gave up your sense of inner power to another. Remember the event and the feelings attached to it in every detail. You may wish to write it down in your Journal. Then re-create that same event in a way that gives you your sense of empowerment back! Be creative, explore and discover how you can regain your personal power and direct your own life.

To accomplish this exercise you may wish to talk directly to the person involved. You may want to write a re-creation of the event in your Journal. Or, you could write another un-mailed letter to the person you feel you gave your power to, perhaps even mail it. Make whatever action you decide to take an extraordinary event to unleash yourself from this initial person who took your sense of personal power from you.

One of my clients decided to complete a "spiritual ritual" to release the hold of the person she felt was controlling her sense of power. She wrote a long letter to the person explaining that while she was a child she could not put into words how she really felt. She told him how she had to give up her own dreams and desires and become a selfless "good little girl" just to gain his love and approval. She wrote that she now demands her own power back and that she no longer will put up with feeling like a "lesser-than" person. After completing her letter, she lit a few candles, read the letter aloud, then burned the letter along with her feelings of powerlessness in a private scared ritual.

The Buddha had wise words to share when he wrote a famous Sutra, or scripture, which teaches one to accept only those things which feel right for oneself and which directs one away from the codependency trap:

> Do not believe in anything simply because you have heard it.
>
> Do not believe in traditions because they have been handed down for many generations.
>
> Do not believe in anything because it is spoken and rumored by many.
>
> Do not believe in anything simply because it is found written in your religious books.
>
> Do not believe in anything merely on the authority of your teachers and elders.
>
> But after observation and analysis, when you find that anything agrees with reason, and is conducive to the good and benefit of one and all, then accept it and live up to it.

Love vs. Codependency

Many times when we are exhibiting codependent behavior, we truly believe we truly believe we are showing our love for another. How wrong this assumption is; for if we have not developed and nourished our *self*-love, we have no love to give. False love in the form of codependent behavior is conditional. "I'll do anything you say, be anything you want" is a conditional statement of non-loving. What are the conditions? That you give back to me in return the nurturing and approval I need when I do what you want me to do. On the other hand, unconditional love says, "I love myself and desire to share that love with you." When you are dealing with your issues of codependency, examine your true feelings regarding unconditional love. Just as important as dealing with anger, fear, and guilt, self-love and love for others becomes paramount when exploring why you gave up your inner power to another. To bring self-love and unconditional love into your healing and recovery program can mean the difference between seeing truth or accepting blindness.

All the answers regarding codependency have not arrived in a neat package waiting to be opened by the therapists of the world, but within the therapeutic field lies a considerable amount of knowledge and understanding as to what codependency looks like in the family system. I like author and counselor Robert Subby's view of codependence: "Codependency is... the force that holds us back from self-actualization, keeps us living out someone else's life script." This definition says it all. Sometimes we cannot put into words exactly why we feel so dependent upon others, it *is* like a force. This force keeps us from living our own dreams, our own path. We literally allow ourselves to be a player in someone's or anyone's life script while negating our own play.

When we enter an intimate relationship with another, we expose ourselves not only to as a woman or a man but also the child within that woman or man. Many of us can identify with our relationship choices over the years as a subconscious maneuver to replace a parent. Our child within longs for love and attention from our parents, most likely one in particular. While we are searching for a loving relationship as an adult many times our inner child is the one leading the search. The old cliché of finding a "girl just like the girl that married dear 'ole Dad" is not so far from the truth! Whether a man or a woman, you are going to continue to be disappointed in your romantic choices as long as you allow your inner child to direct your search for relationships because the child within *is* codependent.

If your own inner power just never quite developed, you may have found yourself in one codependent relationship after another trying to simulate your initial codependent parental bond. When this takes place the "...result too often is a submersion of the *self* in others, to the point of losing sight of it." The result is a codependent adult. There is no reason to feel guilty or bad about being dependent upon another or others to help satisfy your feelings for security and nurturing. It only becomes unhealthy when this submersion of self is the "only" way you receive approval and self-worth.

One alternative to coping with the trails of codependent behavior and constructing a healthy relationship is to start putting yourself and your own needs before those of others. This is not selfish, it is taking care of your *self*. To start, you must take care of your own child within. You can give it the nurturing and acceptance it desired while growing up. Allow your child within to receive all the love and approval it needs so you can make your adult decisions concerning relationships from a place of vision not childish blindness.

To help you feel more in control of your own personal power also begin loving yourself as an adult. Make decisions for yourself which result in your receiving nurturing on all levels—physical, emotional, and spiritual. When more men and women choose to be more in-charge of their lives and their destiny and less dependent upon others as a substitute for self-love, our incidence (or epidemic) of codependent behavior will drastically decline.

When clients ask me how to go about loving themselves more, I tell them to treat themselves as if *they* were the person from which they desired love and attention. In other words, if you are in a relationship in which you feel you are codependent, do for yourself what you feel you do for that other person. In this way, you will be giving yourself the caring, loving, tenderness that you bestow on others but neglect to give to yourself. In her book *Subversive Thoughts, Authentic Passions,* Bonnie Kreps writes poignantly about the necessity of self-nurturing and self-love:

> I would call the relationship with self the most fundamental relationship we have, and the foundation for all others. A balanced and harmonious relationship with one's self is the basis not only for personal autonomy but also for love.... establishing a viable relationship with self is homework at its most basic, not only as each person's life task but as a primary lesson in love.

This lesson in love is a life long effort. From the moment of our birth to the last few minutes of our life, we are trying to figure out who we are and why we are here. Our relationship to our Self is the primary relationship we will have in our lifetime. However, it is also important to realize that self-love is difficult to maintain without outside validation, respect, and affection which affirms our feelings of self-worth. Therefore, a steady source of recognition and nourishment from others helps us to sustain our personal self-love. In this manner, we can balance our inner and outer needs for love and affection. When we learn to love ourselves, we can learn how to ask for what we need from others.

Growing Up Codependent

In Chapter Six, the concept of being slotted or type-cast into a role within the family was introduced. There is another role we are given by our family (and society) which is based on our gender. The socialization of gender identity begins at the moment of birth when the doctor announces, "It's a boy!" or "It's a girl!" At this instant, each infant is treated according to a predetermined sex role.

Gender-role stereotypes are alive and well. Little girls who were programmed to enjoy wearing their fluffy pink dress in the 1950s are still expecting their daughters and grand-daughters to wear the same pink dress. The tough boys of the same era who enjoyed their sports games and rough-housing activity have become the father's who still encourage their sons to enter competitive sports and hide their emotions. As a boy, were you allowed to show your emotions, fears, and pain? As a girl, were you allowed to demonstrate your athletic ability or display your feelings of anger?

Were you expected to follow a set of behaviors and/or emotions because of your gender? If a girl, did your parents treat you differently than your brothers? Or, were you expected to excel in school, clean the house, and cook the family meals? If a boy, were your parents more interested in your ability to play ball than to express yourself verbally or artistically? Was it implied to you that women are the "weaker" sex? Were you told men are the decision-makers? Take a moment to think back to your childhood years and determine if you were raised in an environment which separated the boys from the girls by an accepted type of behavior.

Sex roles are just one of the many programs we buy into as we are growing up which instill codependent behavior. We learned as children that we must act and react in a certain manner depending upon our gender. We were good learners! We adapted to our sex roles and when we complied, we received praise and approval. This results in codependent behavior and many of us continue seeking this pattern of recognition from others well into adulthood. More women than men have been taught to use codependent behavior for in our society women are considered "passive" while men are "aggressive." Our society dictates that women have less power than men, therefore, more women have opted for codependent patterns as a means to satisfy their needs and at the same time appear submissive.

Boys have been raised to feel they must be "one up" on their peers, and others in general, which sustains their "power-over" game. Girls are taught to "give in" and "let the boy decide" which instills powerlessness. The idea of "one-upmanship" can be likened to the saying, "a man is the captain of his own ship" or "a man's home is his castle." This type of thought has been handed down generation after generation to imply that men are the dominate sex while women are submissive. A quote comes to mind which explains the phenomenon of the sex roles: "Men worry about being pushed around; women, about being pushed away." If this is true, we are in trouble!

Ginger was referred to me for depression. She had just recently adopted her second child, a baby girl, and was feeling "out of control" with her emotions. Her mother had died within the last year and she felt this was also contributing to her feelings of frustration and anger. As she related her story to me, I started asking her questions about her childhood, her parents, brothers and sisters. Ginger was the only girl of three children and grew up feeling like she needed to "be one of the boys" in order to be accepted by her father. She described her mother as a "spend-a-holic," spending thousands

of dollars on herself and her home without consulting anyone. It was openly understood that her mother was not considered intelligent or successful by her father or her brothers.
Therefore, as a child Ginger did not identify with her mother,
or her female gender, for there was a fear of being looked
down upon or thought of as "less than." On a subconscious
level, she chose to be more masculine thus trying to please
her father and brothers.

This unconscious choice forced Ginger into a codependent
relationship. She was faced with either being like a boy or
being rejected. Her depression stemmed from not being able
to control her emotions (mostly anger) which was very upsetting and she honestly could not put her finger on why this
was happening. She related a desire to "know what she
wanted and the ability to say it without getting so angry all
the time." She said she was a perfectionist and "I won't start
something unless I know I can finish it and do it top-of-the-
class." Her constant striving for approval from her father and
brothers indicated that Ginger had been molded quite neatly
into the person they wanted her to be, however, she was not
happy with the result.

Ginger "turned-off" her "feminine energy" long ago because her mother was feminine and she did not want to be
like her mother for then she would not "have the respect of
my father and brothers." Now with a new baby to care for she
was confronted with how to relate as a mother and wife—very
feminine roles—and keep her identification as a successful,
capable business person. At this point, Ginger felt she was
"not being who she really was inside." She was caught in a
double-bind situation. She was a woman but internalized
that she must be like a man or forfeit the family acceptance
and approval. In her marriage, Ginger also felt as if she might
lose her husband if she displayed who she really felt herself
to be, which was more feminine.

Ginger's childhood cross-gender identification triggered a
depression which was made conscious by her current situation of needing to be at home to care for her two children.
Once she began Re-Creation Therapy™ and working with her
child within, Ginger soon discovered by herself the "whys" of

her depression. She was eager to explore the techniques and exercises, as well as, the hypnosis sessions to more fully understand how she was misled into a codependent relationship with her father and brothers. By trying to get their love and approval as a child, while at the same time feeling ashamed of her own sex, Ginger literally abandoned her little girl within.

Art therapy, autohypnosis, and emotional release exercises were the means which led Ginger to feel healthy, powerful, and acknowledge her femininity. She discussed her self-discovery with her husband and began sharing her "fears of being rejected" to her father. Once she took that first step of breaking the silence, Ginger lifted her need for codependent behavior and donned a new dress of femininity, capability, and empowerment. She is now a happy mother and wife newly discovering her relationship with her father and brothers as a woman.

When parents and society agree to equal treatment between boys and girls, we may discover hidden talents as "human beings" which we have long buried. You may have hidden childhood dreams to be a sports writer, to bake cakes, become a dancer, doctor, or the President of the United States! These dreams can come to fruition for all men and women when we stop separating the sexes and start supporting all *human beings* and encouraging their individual talents, not gender role stereotypes.

Whether a man or woman, you have been playing your gender roles since the age of two or three years old. This behavior cannot be considered abnormal or pathological. Along with these gender roles, however, many times we do not realize the codependent behavior being continued in adulthood. This codependency can become unhealthy if we neglect taking care of our own needs because we are so wrapped-up in caring for others. What can you do about it? You can move forward and begin to explore your own interpretations of what it means to be female or male. Are you restricting yourself and your childhood dreams because of your gender? Do you think one sex is more powerful than the other? Do you believe women are more sensitive or emotional than men?

If you find that you have continued a sex role to receive the love and approval you need, begin re-creating your beliefs of what a girl/woman and a boy/man can be. Experiment with your feelings regarding your gender and the so-called boundaries they may imply to you. Challenge yourself to develop a more powerful self-purpose no matter what your sex. Establish your own line-of-credit now by utilizing your personal power to ask for what you want and then draw from this private treasury the necessary love and approval needed. Start believing that it is okay to ask for what you want regardless of your gender.

Let me end this Chapter on codependency by sharing an old Sufi story entitled "The Bird and the Egg" which demonstrates quite nicely the strong attachments we have toward our parents and how we learn so aptly our codependent tendencies.

> Once upon a time there was a bird which did not have the power of flight. Like a chicken, he waddled about on the ground, although he knew that some birds did fly.
>
> It so happened that through a combination of circumstances the egg of a flying bird was incubated by this flightless one.
>
> In due time the chick came forth. Instinctively, he knew he had the potentiality for flight.
>
> One day the young bird asked, "When will I fly?"
>
> The land bound bird said, "Persist in your attempts to fly, but do not long for it." He did not know how to take the fledgling out for its lesson in flying or even how to topple it from the nest so it might learn.
>
> The young bird did not understand why his foster-parent could not teach him to fly, but felt much gratitude to this one who had hatched him. "Without my parent," the young bird said to himself, "surely I would still be in the egg!"
>
> He pondered, "Anyone who can hatch me, surely can teach me to fly. It must be just a matter of time;

or perhaps, it's my own fault that I cannot fly because I am not worthy."

"I know," he said aloud, "suddenly, one day I will be carried to the next stage by the one who has brought me thus far. It will be like a miracle and my parent will use all his wisdom and magic to help me fly on my own."

And so he waited....

Child Within Exercises

1. Let's face it, how many of us felt completely loved and accepted for who we were as a child? I surmise, not many. You have the choice to keep your feelings of non-acceptance, bringing them out of the closet now and then to display to others like a badge: "I was never loved as a child. My parents whipped me and always put me down." You also have the choice to let go of and re-create these feelings of "not living up to your parents' expectations." If you feel you did everything as a child to try to please your parents but always "fell short," explore with your inner child the ages and experiences which generated these feelings. Was it because you wanted to be or do other things than your gender socially allowed at the time? Or, were you just too busy trying to please your parents that you could not cultivate your own interests?

If you were told as a child, "Only sissies cry" or "Young ladies don't play football," you can change those acquired beliefs to more clearly represent your present feelings toward behaviors which limit your gender. It is never too late to start a new project, sport, or activity. Try completing one new task this month. Begin a class, write a poem, paint a picture, sculpt a piece of pottery, run in a race, learn to knit, take up any activity which you could not do as a child because it was considered "not appropriate" for your gender. Today you can do and become anything you desire. You can rid yourself of leftover sex role stereotyping by engaging in an "action" which you choose to explore but were taught as a child went against your gender classification. Allow yourself to be free from past constricting childhood sex role identifications and you will observe your codependent tendencies begin to fade.

2. As a child, did you create turmoil to arouse the attention you desired? Many times this behavior becomes locked into our adult patterns of relating to others. While growing up in a dysfunctional family system, it may have become necessary to use diverse tactics to gain recognition. One of these methods is acting in a codependent fashion. Examine

your present beliefs surrounding intimate relationships and what they mean to you. Does a relationship mean:

__ having the ability to hold and comfort another?

__ the ability to give and receive?

__ sharing with a person you can trust?

__ a situation where you feel trustworthy?

__ being able to share secrets without fear?

__ a sense of fear in being rejected?

__ having someone to listen to you?

__ needing to take care of someone?

__ knowing you will be taken care of?

When you have written down in your Journal what an intimate relationship means to you, go down the list and note where and when you adopted these perspectives. You may be surprised at just how many assumptions and feelings come directly from your childhood. We pattern much of our own relationships from what we witnessed and experienced as a child. To check your tendency for codependent behavior, go back down the list and put a mark by any response which indicates your "giving up your personal power to another." These beliefs are the ones to examine and re-create in the subsequent autohypnosis and in your present relationships.

3. Today's liberal culture still pressures little boys to become strong and aggressive and its girls to be passive, quiet, and alluring. The truth is we all have feminine and masculine qualities within us. Delve into the forbidden emotions, events, actions, and thoughts of your opposite sex self. You can relearn that you are a whole person possessing dual natures of feminine and masculine qualities. In your Journal make two lists. Heading the first list write "feminine" and the other "masculine." Beneath each heading write down all the emotions, events, thoughts, behaviors, and so forth which you feel are predominantly male or female.

Now recheck each list to see if you can take any of the items from one list and add it to the other list. Lastly, cross-off the items which are now on both lists. Those items which are left on each list are your current beliefs toward the duality of male and female. These ingrained childhood beliefs can be re-created by discovering the incidents in your childhood which instilled them. Ask your child within at what age you learned each particular notion, go back into autohypnosis visualization to discover how this belief came about, then re-create it to conform with how you choose to relate today as an adult to what it means to be a man or a woman. Re-create each item on your list which you believe is more limiting to that gender than you would like it to be.

4. In this Chapter, I spoke of a client who used a "ritual" to help release the emotional ties to a person from her past which she felt had controlled her. Rituals can be a splendid means in achieving a solid foundation with oneself and reality. They are activities which one creates to use as a type of re-identification with one's personal power. They can be anything from simple daily prayer and meditation to the purification ceremony of burning sage; or perhaps more lengthy rituals, such as drawing figures in the sandy lake or ocean shore, or hiking in the woods on a regular basis. Whatever you choose for your ritual, it will help you see yourself and your life more clearly. Make it an enjoyable endeavor, one in which you look forward to each time you undergo it. Also, your personal ritual can be changed when you feel the need to move on to a more fresh, more in-depth sense of exploration.

Rituals do not necessarily need be religious or spiritual, nor do they need to cost anything. Make your ritual as simple or as complex as you wish. When much of your life is surrounded with entertaining or caring for others in a typical codependent fashion, a personal ritual can bring that much desired union with the Self. In undergoing personal ritual, you can become more "in-tune" with your personal inner power by taking charge of your relationship with your Self. These self-empowering rituals can reveal the strong yet magical sense of self which you are becoming.

Child Within Affirmations

I accept myself as a perfect creation combining both feminine and masculine.

I am free to experience my life both intuitively and logically.

I possess personal power.

I choose to care for myself as I care for others.

Child Within Autohypnosis

Lie down and relax. Close your eyes. Let your mind travel to the beautiful sights and sounds of a lush forest. Smell the dew drops on the green leaves and mint scrub around you. Sense the life hidden in the trees above you and the rocks below. Listen to the deep noises from within the night's darkness and perceive the powerful force lying dormant within. Continue walking forward into the night air and feel its breath stroke your cheek. Search with your eyes the path beneath your feet and watch it twist and turn as it winds its way around rocks and trees, waterfalls and streams. Follow your feet as they take you further and further into the moonlit forest.

Through the moonlight you find a clearing, a large circle. Sit down Indian-style in the middle of this enclosed area. Close you eyes and sense within your body a place of *power*. This place may be in your stomach, chest, or even your head. Wherever your place of power resides, go there....

Feel the energy coming from this center of empowerment within you. It feels strong, magical, and full of Light. With this powerful sensation allow your child within to help you remember a time in your childhood when you did *not* feel powerful. Get in touch with the emotions you felt when you were this age and in this position of powerlessness. Watch for who is with you in this situation of the past and what was happening to make you feel defenseless and vulnerable.

Now gently re-create this scene using all your new-found personal power acquired from your walk in the mighty forest. You may wish to perform a ritual to unleash your feelings of powerlessness. Perhaps seeing yourself lighting a candle to purify the incident then watching the flame diminish into nothingness. When you have successfully released any feelings of helplessness, re-create your emotions into feelings of strength and wholeness....

Upon completing your re-creation, open your eyes to find yourself sitting within the forest clearing once again with the sun of a new day gleaming down upon your face. Feel this warm glowing energy touch the place of power within your body. Now return to total awareness filled with a new sense of personal empowerment and strength.

(Take a moment to write in your Journal about your experience with this empowering autohypnosis.)

Child Within Journal

Child Within Journal

8   The Saboteurs

"Nothing is at last sacred but the integrity of your own mind."
—Ralph Waldo Emerson

There are four human emotions which can inhibit, stagnate, stifle, and weaken our progress to heal physically, emotionally, and spiritually. They each hang like dark gray clouds over our existence, shrouding our freedom of choice, hiding our truth, and blocking our Light. These four emotional saboteurs are *fear, anger, guilt,* and *shame.*

We have all experienced these four emotions at some time in our lives, therefore, I will not explain or define them. Instead, I am going to relate four stories that correlate with each of these saboteurs. As you read the four client cases, test yourself by trying to associate what you read with your own feelings relating to fear, anger, guilt, and shame. Examine if or how you let your emotions sabotage your choices, activities, and relationships as an adult. As you are reading about these very real "saboteurs," explore if and when you first began sabotaging your life and goals with fear, anger, guilt or shame. Just as a dark cloud looks as if it were never going to go away, it rises upward then disappears into the sky. Like that cloud, you can learn to lift the pain of fear, anger, guilt, and shame which has been sabotaging your integrity.

Fear is Feeling Powerless

A baby's first cry of life is filled with fear. It knows nothing else but to voice the pain of a scary entrance into an unknown world. Many times, the last breath of a person's life is also filled with this powerless fear. We humans have devised hundreds of fears to contend with in our short existence—from the fear of birth to the fear of death. Fear *can* become crippling in its effects.

Sadly, most people presume fear is a necessary part of daily life. They contend we must be alert, cautious, and a bit fearful of those people and circumstances which might harm us. A national poll revealed 53% of the people polled did not trust others. This opposing cycle of fear instructs: Defend yourself against those things and persons which may harm you, be defensive and ready to take action or to run. The "fight or flight" response is typical of how we react to our fears in many situations. But what about our fears which we feel we cannot fight or flee, such as the fear of pain, abandonment, or death?

Fear lasts only as long as you give it permission. Whenever you have a fear which is unapproachable, look beyond it and research the *underlying reason* for it. Do not allow fear to inflict its shadow of powerlessness upon you. Fear can be recognized for what it is shielding and then that issue or emotion can be confronted. Gerald Jampolsky spoke of the need to extinguish the cycle of fear when he wrote, "*Love* is letting go of fear." He implies here that the "power of love" can triumph over mistrust and fear.

Eric was a handsome man in his late thirties when he first came to me for therapy because of a chronic fear of death. When he was growing up, Eric had a terrible fear of his parents dying, as well as, he himself dying young. While his mother did die when he was sixteen years old, his father lived to be almost ninety. Now with the recent death of his father, Eric's persistent fear of death was being challenged. He also believed his fear of death was causing many physical maladies he was currently experiencing—heart palpitations, low energy, pains in his stomach, and high levels of anxiety. At this same time, Eric was encountering a new awareness in his spirituality and was challenging his childhood beliefs by questioning if there really was a Higher Power, God.

Eric talked of needing to put "a cap on his emotions" for fear of letting them all out and then being left with nothing inside. He was a sensitive, caring man who required "permission" to explore his emotions. He told me his father had been an unemotional man and that as a young boy he learned how to keep his feelings to himself. His father's recent death was forcing him to review his life and confront his emotions.

Along with several weeks of stress management exercises to curb anxiety, the use of autohypnosis tapes and guided visualizations, I regressed Eric to explore his child within. During one age regression to seven years old, Eric told of how he had to sleep in the same room as his mother, father, and sister. His family lived in the desert and there were no neighbors for many miles. He slept in an upper bunk and could look out into the dark desert night through a small window by his head which gave him a "small sense of security." He felt as if he was all alone in a big dry land and described his childhood as "barren."

Another age regression session uncovered his five year old child within. During a hot summer day, Eric experienced a fall on his tricycle and cut his face badly. His father asserted, "It doesn't hurt" and showed very little affection or concern. This remembered incident initiated a strong emotional release from Eric and he proceeded to hold his stomach tightly while still under hypnosis. I asked him where in his body he felt the fear of death and he responded, "It's like a knot in my stomach." At this point, I encouraged Eric to release his feelings of fear. This fear was exposed to be the fear of being abandoned (desert-ed) as a young child and left in the hot *desert* to die.

I asked Eric to begin soothing his stomach area with his hands and to imagine himself going to the rescue of his five year old child right after the tricycle fall. He told me of how he was able to pickup the small child and "carry him close to his heart" calming and reassuring him. He told me of his ability to talk to his child within and tell him he would "grow up to be strong and healthy and live a long life." Eric told his child within he would take care of him and he need not be afraid any longer. He re-created the entire incident and later wrote it down in his Journal.

Eric's fear of dying was manifesting a "slow death" for him as an adult, however, with the aid of his child within, he was able to understand the initial "whys" of his fear and subsequently let it go. Eric learned that he no longer needed to sabotage his desires with his fears or let them destroy him physically. He continued working with his child within and his fear of death soon disappeared. At the same time, he expanded his views regarding religion and began talking as if there really were a Higher Power after all. He joined a community church and began searching for new direction and support.

Anger Is False Power

Many of us associate the *emotion* of anger with the *action* of violence. This is an erroneous association. Anger can be expressed in a variety of modes all of which do not include violent behavior. It is *repressed* anger which can cause one to become aggressively violent or even manifest physically in the form of illness. When we choose not to voice our angry feelings but instead choose to harbor them within us, we initiate a *sense of false power* for we are not able to do or say what we want or need. Repressed anger is false power which results in fear, powerlessness.

If we release our anger constructively, without malice, we can also release the relenting fear attached to it. Letting go of anger in a healthy fashion could mean talking through a disagreement, writing a letter to clear the point in question, taking a long walk, pounding a pillow, or sitting and meditating. Each of these and other modes of dispelling anger can become an avenue which leads to its resolution. However, *if your anger remains silent, it becomes powerless fear which can accumulate and multiply over a lifetime.*

Sharon came to me saying she had been in and out of therapy most of her life but still felt she needed to experience a "deep emotion buried inside." She said she came from a "dysfunctional family, which I think is really crazy." Her father was ninety-three years old and "dying" and her mother was eighty-three in good health. Sharon related that her childhood was "sad" and does not remember much joy or happiness at all while growing up. Her mother and father had many fights and were not demonstrative in their affection for each other or their daughters.

Sharon suffered from a "spastic colon" for most of her adult life with medical tests revealing nothing abnormal. She also stated that she could not urinate in a public restroom for fear of other women "hearing her." She did not know why she felt this way. During the initial meeting of her inner child in hypnosis, Sharon found a "sad little girl who could not cry or laugh." She was unable to touch or hug her child within but did talk to her and reassured her that she would return. Following up with several guided visualizations, Sharon could only find lonely, fearful, angry scenes throughout her childhood.

I asked Sharon if she could think of a reason why she would not allow herself to be happy. I suggested that perhaps there was something she was getting out of not being healthy and free to be herself, a secondary gain. She revealed a tremendous insight saying, "Then I would have to be happy and I wouldn't know how to act or who to be." Also, she believed if she were happy and free somehow it would be taken away from her and she "just couldn't go through that *again*." I asked her if she had experienced what this felt like and she said, "Yes. I just couldn't go through the pain of being happy and having it all taken away." I inquired how long it had been since she had experienced a caring relationship; she told me four years and that she had no interest in pursuing one.

I used age regression with Sharon beginning first with a pleasant year which we had previously discussed, she was twenty-six years old and living in Europe for a year. It was the only time she could remember that she had any fun or sense of freedom in her entire life (Sharon was in her early fifties when she first came to see me). I instructed her to visualize and experience in her mind everything about her stay overseas. She was to smell the air, taste the food, sense the feelings, see the landscape, and hear the sounds around her. Then gently, I counted her down in an age regression to her childhood years stopping at age four. She described her home, mother, father, and sister to me. The scene was not a happy one. There was much pressure, work, and illness. Her father worked little and controlled the family with his con-

tinuous orders from a nearby couch. Her mother took care of
the farm and most of the work.

Slowly counting up to ten years old, Sharon witnessed her
illness at this age and said, "it feels like mono (meaning
mononucleosis) and I am in bed and very weak." Bringing her
up to age twelve, she related how she started her menstrual
period and thought she was bleeding to death. "It was an
awful experience, nothing was ever said to me about it before
it came and little after. I guess mom just figured it out and
showed me where the pads were." The area of natural bodily
functions was very "dirty and bad." This became evident in
Sharon's fear of urinating in public places and the embar-
rassment and fear of intimate relationships. I ended the session with counting her up to age twenty-six once again,
instilling that she had in fact experienced happiness in her
life and had the choice to do so again. Finally, Sharon was
counted up to her present age with instructions that she
remember her hypnosis experience.

Soon Sharon's physical body was responding to the positive hypnosis suggestions. She also listened to hypnosis
audiocassettes at home which I had made for her to encourage relaxation and enhance her ability for deeper age regression sessions. Her colon was functioning more appropriately
and she was beginning to view herself with a certain degree
of freedom. We talked of her depression, anger, and apathy.
She shared many nightmares and dreams which frightened
her. She also shared her desire to "have someone to be myself with, but I don't trust anyone." At this point, I held her
and let her cry in my arms and reassured her I would support her emotions and her decisions. She said no one had
ever done that before and agreed to work with her child
within on a regular basis.

During one session, Sharon related an incident when she
was seven years old. She was riding home from the opera
with her mother and aunt who had told her not to use the
restroom at the theater because it was "dirty." She was
squirming in the backseat and finding it increasingly more
difficult to "hold it." Finally, after much insistence that she
could no longer wait to urinate, her mother pulled off the side

of the road and proceeded to tell her to go right there on the ground by the car. This memory triggered another incident of her mother giving her enemas and how she always had stomach aches and many times even vomited. At this point, Sharon's anger with her mother finally exploded. I asked Sharon to speak to me as if I was her mother and to tell me what she was feeling. The dam of repressed anger poured forth. Her anger also addressed her father's behavior who controlled her and made her feel "unworthy."

Following this release of anger toward her mother and father, I instructed Sharon to re-create the scene with her mother and aunt at the theater to one she could feel good about. In her re-creation she was able to use the restroom when necessary and feel clean and feminine doing so. Then I asked her to take the available crayons and construction paper and draw a picture of herself as a child. Her drawing was labeled "dread" and was of a figure with its back arched and heavily burdened. There was a block or wall around the entire drawing like a dark bubble, this she related was her protection. She had kept in her anger to protect herself. With more direction, Sharon was able to draw an opening in the far side of the bubble as a beginning to letting her anger out.

When I asked her to draw the anger which was being released, Sharon quickly picked up a black and a red crayon and let her anger erupt. She even began ripping the pages of the pad pressing down harder and harder. When she was finished, she started to laugh and said how good it felt to let it out. I told her to take the pages home with her and burn them in a ritual of letting her anger go. A few months later, Sharon chose to confront her parents with her feelings of being abused as a child.

Sharon is continuing her therapy to work with her child within and to heal her real physical wounds of childhood. Some of the insights Sharon shared with me about working with her child within were never being able to voice her "disgust with her parents quite so profusely;" realizing just how controlling her parents were in her childhood and how she was still allowing them to control her life; and, how she still wanted her parents' love and approval.

Guilt is Dressed in Disapproval

Guilt comes dressed in an array of attire, however, sewn on each inside label is the word, "Disapproval." When we feel the emotion of guilt there is a disapproving catalyst somewhere to be found. Whether the disapproval comes from society, cultural philosophy, friends, parents, family members, or ourselves, it spurs our concept of what is to be accepted in our environment and what is not. When we were children, guilt was dressed in many costumes, from religious cloaks to aprons strings and from silent suits to loud sharp hats. Even our own disapproval of nakedness may have been a disguise for guilt.

As we mature and "grow up," these same disapproving ensembles fill our wardrobe until we rid ourselves of the guilt which they are concealing. Repressed guilt is *unhealthy guilt,* guilt which keeps us law-abiding and productive could be called *healthy guilt.* There will always be a certain degree of unhealthy guilt if we let ourselves believe we are not approved of by others, or ourselves. As psychologist and author Joan Borysenko wrote in her book *Guilt is the Teacher, Love is the Lesson,* "Unhealthy guilt causes life to become organized around the need to avoid fear rather than the desire to share love.... In guilt we say no to life." If we continually live under the guise of unhealthy guilt, we assume a tendency to become defensive, employing self-protection at every opportunity which sabotages the very goals and desires for which we are striving.

Is it time to clean out your closets and toss away the old, outdated dress of disapproval, guilt? This is exactly what Susan decided to do. I began seeing Susan for an overall feeling of low self-worth. She was a light-hearted sort of person and I found her to be in quite happy spirits during most of our sessions together. She was a small woman with a girlish presentation, both verbally and physically. Immediately, she expressed a desire to feel successful in her career, which she did not. This was disturbing her but she was not quite sure how to get past the heavy, almost "guilty feelings" which accompanied her goals to succeed. She also related that she had difficulty finding and staying in a relationship with a "straight, clean man." New relationships would start with her feeling accepted and appreciated only to end in disappointing renunciation.

After bringing in photographs of her family to share with me, I asked Susan to draw a picture of herself as a child in her Journal. The picture she drew was of a very masculine child of ten years old shown only from the waist up. Her hair was cut very short like a boy's crew-cut. She was wearing a stripped T-shirt; she had two empty eye sockets, no mouth or lower face; and a big pink heart placed at her left shoulder. Obviously, Susan's perception of herself as a child was in conflict with how she presented herself as an adult, which was very feminine. She stated that her self-concept as a child had always been low because she never felt she measured-up to her father's expectations.

Susan's first hypnosis meeting with her child within took place near a cave at the ocean. She was able to hold her little girl and talk with her. I asked Susan if her child within had anything she wanted to tell us and she shouted, "I hate Daddy!" I directed Susan to confront her child within and explain that it was okay for her to share her feelings. After the hypnosis, Susan shared she had felt guilty about hating her father while growing up because he never thought she was smart or could become anything worthwhile. She proceeded to write in her Journal beneath her drawing, "I hate myself. I want to die." We worked with Susan's lack of self-worth by having her re-create several events of her childhood in which she felt she was not successful or intelligent enough to complete her projects. She explained to me that as a child each time she thought she was doing something successful her father would "put her down" in some fashion.

During the next age regression, I asked Susan to meet with her child within at the ocean and to have her father join them. Susan was able to guide a conversation between her child within and her father. This communication went on for several minutes until everything Susan's inner child needed to tell her father was voiced. In the end, Susan was able to re-create herself, her child within, and her father playing joyously together on the sandy shore. Upon gaining full conscious awareness, Susan remarked how free she felt, as if something had been lifted.

Previously, as an adult, Susan did not like to visit her father for it activated her old feelings of rejection and guilt which she had felt as a child. A few sessions later, Susan shared with me she had visited her father and talked to him about her guilt feelings of "not living up to his expectations." She told him, "I just want you to be proud of me." He acknowledged her and responded that he understood and attempted a soft hug. Susan was in seventh heaven! She decided to work by herself with her inner child on other areas pertaining to her mother. Susan informed me several weeks later that she had left a destructive relationship and her career was beginning to move forward. She was in the process of releasing her disapproving guilt.

Shame is Self-Hatred

Which words induced a response of shame within you as a child? Perhaps like many, the words, "Thou shalt not" or "Shame on you" bring painful feelings of shame to the surface. Or, maybe the impelling words, "You're no good" or "You should be ashamed of yourself" accompanied with an accusing finger brings the arousal of shame's self-loathing. When we are placed in the line of shame's fire, we soon realize what it means to feel the flames of self-hate.

Author and lecturer John Bradshaw states in his book *Healing The Shame That Binds You*, "Without the healthy signal of shame, we would not be in touch with our core dependency needs" and goes on to explain that we need a certain amount of *self-induced* shame to signal our desire for help. Bradshaw's projected claim of a "healthy" shame is difficult for me to envision. Healthy guilt, (to keep us law-abiding and/or "to signal our desire for help") I can relate to, however, healthy shame I cannot. What can be healthy about hating yourself which is what shame is all about?

Bradshaw's contribution to the recovery field in the area of shame-based families and shame-based behavior in childhood is commendable and I am most grateful for his insight.

However, his instruction on healthy and unhealthy shame can be challenged. If a young child begins feeling ashamed of himself because of what was done to him physically or emotionally, or, if he assumes the blame for his family members' actions by self-inducing shameful feelings, that young child is procuring someone else's "internal guilt." As Bradshaw himself states, "Guilt says I made a mistake, while shame says I *am* a mistake." With this distinction, is it really necessary to have *any kind of shame* present in our lives? There may be a fine line between feeling guilty and the feelings of being ashamed of oneself; however, the first can signal the need for guidance without employing the second, which only brings self-hatred.

Shame is contagious. While growing up, we seem to accumulate shame, stuffing it deep within our subconscious mind. Shame enters our lives through many avenues. If you feel unwanted by your parents, you feel ashamed. If you are humiliated in public, you feel ashamed. If your drawings and papers from school are ignored, you feel ashamed. If your parents did not attend the school functions you wanted them to go to, you feel ashamed. If your parents' socioeconomic level is not that of your friends, you feel ashamed. If you are blamed or teased for having "bad" habits, you feel ashamed. Obviously, the list is never-ending and unnecessary. No child should ever feel the pain of shame's self-hatred.

As erroneous as it might sound, children often take on the shame of their parents. A past client named Julie asked for help to explore her feelings of being ashamed. She said she had experienced an underlying sense of shame throughout her life. She felt the shame was related to her body and her uncontrollable temper flare-ups. Julie was a successful business woman, married happily, but could not verify a concrete reason for her feelings of shame. Julie's mother was alive and well, her father had died about one year earlier. She told me the relationship between her mother and father never really seemed to include love. She never saw them hug or kiss and grew up feeling as if her mother felt guilty about her own sexuality.

Julie said she also had deep-seeded feelings of anger which would surface now and then, but felt they were "misdi-rected." She would find herself "over-reacting" by shouting and yelling when she really did not want to. After the initial reaching steps of Re-Creation Therapy™, I guided Julie on an age regression journey back to meet her child within. Julie easily met her child within whose little body frame was "hunched-over with big sad eyes and straight oily hair that looked like it was never combed." (Julie later informed me she had a severe spinal-curvature which had developed in childhood and was now quite visible as an adult.)

Before the next hypnosis session, Julie spoke about her mother's lack of compassion and empathy toward her when she was growing up. She felt as if her mother continually "put her down and criticized her." As adults, they were still relating poorly. Julie also shared that she experienced forced routine enemas at the hands of her mother. She expressed this with great disgust and recounted there was "much pain and a sense of invasion." I supported these feelings and ac-knowledged that these incidents of force were comparable to being raped.

During the following age regression, Julie was able to reach a very young child within, barely old enough to talk. I asked Julie to use her ability to communicate with her inner child at this age and tell me what she was feeling. She re-sponded that she felt ashamed. I asked her what she was ashamed of and she proceeded to tell me "because my mother put her finger into me and I feel naughty." Julie's memory of this traumatic experience had not previously been consciously remembered. This new information ushered in an awareness of where Julie's shame and repressed anger had originated. Julie recognized that as a young child she had taken on her mother's guilt and shame about her body by instilling her own sense of shame and self-hatred.

Julie had carried her feelings of shame many years, from her earliest childhood. Other painful memories of incestuous events were soon disclosed in therapy and each time it was mentioned or discussed, I asserted that "she had nothing to be ashamed of and that at the time she had had no control over the situation." Her anger toward her mother began to surface at this same time which aided her in releasing both emotions, her deep-seeded anger and her shame. It was also speculated that Julie's early spinal malformation started in her infancy with the automatic reaction of curling in a ball (the fetal position) while sleeping to protect herself from possible probing intrusions.

I encouraged Julie to re-create her many childhood memories which were now flooding her consciousness. Through the help of an assortment of counseling methods, Julie began to discern how she had acquired her mother's shameful feelings about her body and her sexuality. Since she still held much of this shame as an adult, I directed Julie to sit in a chair across from three pillows propped-up on the couch facing her. I asked her to talk to each of the pillows opposite her as if they were her father, mother, and her child within. She proceeded to tell each of her parents how angry she was at them for their actions and behaviors during her childhood. The shame her mother caused her was discussed and the guilt of hating her father was let go. Julie was able to tell each of them exactly how she felt and release many repressed emotions. She was also able to allow her child within to sit between her parents and talk with each of them. When the exercise was complete, Julie realized she need not feel ashamed of anything done to her as a child against her will.

Recognizing and Slaying the Saboteurs

Growing up in a family that serves an alcoholic's ego is not an easy task. All the attention is directed toward the alcoholic. As in any dysfunctional family where a parent is dependent on a substance or obsessed with a certain behavior, the family members take a backseat in all respects. My childhood feelings of fear, anger, guilt, and shame are obvious to me as I reflect back to my childhood. Recognizing the saboteurs can be easy if you listen to your inner child's guidance. I can close my eyes and remember fear instilling nightmares which were not comforted; misunderstandings inducing anger that were not resolved; guilt-producing activity which was kept silent; and shameful feelings that were never recognized or abated. I learned all too young that my feelings and emotions were not very important.

My father was a closet alcoholic, recovering the last twelve years of his life. He would drink alone, believing he kept his secret from us. I think the first time I truly realized my father was an alcoholic was not until I was a teenager; however, the effects of his drinking during my younger years is most evident to me. Expectedly, my self-esteem and self-worth was greatly affected by the lack of approval I received during those growing up years. Also, I can trace back to my childhood the very saboteurs which kept me from succeeding in my young adulthood.

One very real scene which I have re-created several times is the "coming home routine." I would wait eagerly for my father to come home from work at night and run to greet him with a hug and a kiss only to find him very "busy" in the garage. He would brush me off with a comment to go help mother with dinner. This obvious rejection was the result of his "solo trips" into his bottle. I kept up this "coming home routine" for several years and each time I felt unloved, hurt, and confused. These three feelings then turned to anger, guilt, and fear—anger that he was rejecting me and guilt and fear that maybe I was not "good enough" to be his daughter.

Another memory I have regarding shame was during my teen years. I never wanted to invite any of my girlfriends over to our house for fear they would see my Dad in a drunken state. Not to say he was a cruel man when he was drinking, just the opposite; he became the "mushy nice guy." I was just ashamed of him when he was drinking. I had taken on shame for something I did not do. I sabotaged myself many times throughout my adolescence with my feelings of being ashamed "for" my father. I carried this emotional shame with me into adulthood until I realized how I had assumed my *father's* guilt and shame. I then recognized I had done nothing to warrant the feelings I had carried with me for so long.

Fear, anger, guilt, and shame, the four saboteurs. Have you witnessed any or all of these emotions sabotaging your goals? Do thoughts of fear or guilt enter your mind just when you think you are reaching the top? Does anger rage inside you but you cannot put your finger on just why? Are there times when you feel so ashamed that you no longer feel worthy? Examine your inner feelings regarding each of these saboteurs, search for their initial beginnings, then process through them. If they are allowed to stay buried within you, you will find yourself sabotaging even the highest intentions. Do not allow the subconscious secrets of your past to sabotage your future.

When one has lived in a family system which does not allow all of its members to speak freely and be supported emotionally, one becomes very apt at repressing many feelings, the joyous ones as well as the unhappy or fearful emotions. As children, we are quick learners. If a situation instigates a certain emotional response the first time it was experienced but that response was not accepted by our parents, we learn to "repress" that emotion. After repressing a certain emotion throughout our childhood, it becomes easy to veer away from it in adulthood. With this self-limiting emotional expression, however, we may also learn to repress other feelings, such as compassion, joy, excitement, and love.

Author and Transpersonal Therapist Frances Vaughan wrote in her enlightening book *Awakening Intuition*, "Often feelings are repressed because they are painful. But when you repress painful feelings you inevitably repress other feelings, reducing your capacity for experience and closing off vital parts of yourself." A person, whether six years old or sixty years old, has a prerogative to express whatever emotions he or she feels, that includes the saboteurs (fear, anger, guilt and shame). What becomes important is to be able to recognize "what" emotions you are feeling and "why." For if you can name it, you can decide if it is appropriate for the situation at hand. If you find the emotion is not appropriate, you can learn to slay it.

If, however, an emotion is repressed it is not recognized. It does not go away but many times is acted out in other more negative ways such as the "silent treatment," yelling and screaming, or perhaps other more violent behaviors. It has been said that any emotion, if felt and faced, will automatically reveal its message. The facing of an emotion may be a difficult task but when followed through can lead to an understanding of what that emotion represents, what its message may be. Once you understand the message the emotion changes, for all e-motions are in motion.

The following autobiographical parable illustrates perfectly the predicament in which many of us find ourselves when facing the saboteurs of fear, anger, guilt, and shame. The last sentence reveals how we can slay our own personal saboteurs.

Autobiography in Five Short Chapters
Chapter 1
I walk down the street. There is a deep hole in the sidewalk and I fall in. I am lost. I am helpless. It is not my fault. It takes me forever to find a way out.

Chapter 2
I walk down the same street. There is a deep hole in the sidewalk. I pretend I do not see it. I fall in again. I cannot believe I am in the same place, but it is not my fault. It still takes me a long time to get out.

Chapter 3
I walk down the same street. There is a deep hole in the sidewalk. I see it. I still fall in. It is a habit, but my eyes are open and I know where I am. It is my fault. I get out quickly.

Chapter 4
I walk down the same street. There is a deep hole in the sidewalk. I walk around it.

Chapter 5
I walk down a different street.

Child Within Exercises

1. Explore and consciously recognize your fears as an adult. You may have a fear of heights, closed areas, intimacy, success, loneliness, or death. You may already recognize a fear that began in your childhood which you have not been able to fully process as yet. Take this time to begin processing each fear by learning its origin and what emotion is attached to it. Lie down and close your eyes while at the same time concentrating on your fear. Focusing only on your fear, let yourself relax enough to feel the fear physically in your body. Find the place in your body where the fear resides.

Now, place your hand on that area. Just as Eric felt his fear "like a knot in his stomach" you may feel your fear in your stomach area. Perhaps the fear lies hidden in your back, or pulsating in your head. Wherever your fear dwells, go to it. Explore the feelings you encounter. Are the feelings painful? Do they make you angry? Is it a cold or hot feeling? Does your fear feel like guilt? Do you feel powerless? Let yourself *feel* your fear.

Clearly feeling the emotion attached to your fear, put a name on it. When you can give it a name, an emotion, it turns from intangible to tangible. Now let yourself express this emotion. Eric's fear turned into anger which he was able to constructively release. Allow yourself to let go of the emotion which your fear ultimately turned out to represent. Remember, you are releasing a "fear" as you allow yourself to express the emotion attached to it.

Write this experience down in your Journal. Re-create your fear and the emotion attached to it by reviewing the event in your childhood which instigated it. Once again, close your eyes and count yourself down to a certain age as a child. You will automatically stop at the age which is appropriate for you to discover from where your fear originated. Witness the event in which your fear began, then count yourself back up to your present age. You may choose to re-create your experience by using autohypnosis and guided visualization, or by writing it down in your Journal. By recognizing where and why your fear began and by putting a name on the emotion it is eluding, the fear becomes easy to slay.

2. Dealing with anger does not need to be a difficult task. The first rule-of-thumb is to check if your anger is being "misdirected." As in Sharon's case, she knew her anger was not healthy but found she could not keep it under control. If you find you are sabotaging your relationships, career, or goals with covert anger, examine the origin of your emotional rage. Perhaps, as with Sharon, your anger is but a tiny part of the repressed feelings which lie buried inside.

Art therapy is a great way to help dispel anger. With some big crayons and a large pad of paper on the floor in front of you, proceed to close your eyes and enter a light autohypnosis. Relax your body and mind and allow yourself to go to the event or situation which stirs your angry emotions. Knowing only you are the one who will witness your reactions, let yourself feel your anger as it seeps into your body. Just when you think you cannot contain any more anger, open your eyes and pick up a crayon and begin to scribble your feelings down on the paper. Let your hand automatically direct your emotions. Do not try to actually draw a picture or anything comprehendible. Just allow yourself to release your pent-up anger onto the paper. Continue in this manner on as many pages of paper as necessary until you feel you have released your anger appropriately.

You may find yourself a bit depleted of energy by employing this method of emotional release. Take a moment to rest and consciously acknowledge how you have processed through your anger. You may wish to repeat this exercise to totally release your feelings of anger. This exercise can also be completed with other emotions as well. Allow yourself a few days in between each exercise to discern the results. There are many enlightened therapists using art therapy which would be happy to help guide you in your exploration of releasing anger in this way.

3. Growing up with guilt or shame can sabotage you in many ways as an adult. It brings with it low self-esteem and a sense of self-hatred which can eat away at the very core of your being. If you are ready to release the guilt and shame

you have carried in your life, try this exercise. Sit down on a chair and in front of you place another chair or two which represent the persons which have caused you feelings of guilt or shame. As in Julie's process, tell each person exactly how you feel. Tell them why you feel ashamed and how their be-havior instigated these feelings. Let your anger and pain speak out to them. If necessary, allow your child within to also tell them his or her feelings.

When you have communicated all your emotions, sit qui-etly for a few minutes to reflect on what has transpired. Did you touch upon the reasons for your shameful feelings? Were you able to relate you true feelings? Was another person's guilt or shame involved? Write your findings down in your Journal, then take a long walk or run to help disperse any other pent-up energy. Releasing repressed emotions may make you feel a bit drained or you may feel pleasantly exhila-rated. Allow any new emotions to form in the place of the ones you just released, this will help to re-create your per-ceptions of self-worth. A healing has begun. You are walking down a different street!

Child Within Affirmations

I allow myself to feel all my emotions.

It is okay for me to feel angry.

I let my fears go so I may feel my true personal power.

I feel healthy emotionally, physically, and spiritually.

I am willing to release my repressed emotions.

I take action to clear myself of repressed emotions.

Child Within Autohypnosis

Lie down and get comfortable, close your eyes. Breathing slowly and rhythmically allow yourself to completely relax. As in the other autohypnosis exercises, tell each of your muscles to relax and go limp. When you are completely relaxed begin to imagine you are looking out a large picture window. Let yourself imagine anything you want to see. It could be a meadow scene complete with a cool water creek below. You could imagine a cottage or country farm overlooking a massive landscape. It might be that you imagine the blue-green ocean with its shoreline reaching endlessly for miles and miles. Whatever you imagine through the picture window is okay.

You will clearly get in touch with a time in your childhood which you felt a very strong emotion. As in a movie film, have your child within (between the ages of five and ten years old) enter the scene in the picture window. He or she is experiencing a past childhood event which took place many years ago. Watch him or her go through the motions, the behavior that took place which caused this strong emotion. There may be other people in the scene, bring them there if necessary. Allow the flood of memories regarding this event to form clearly in your mind. There is no need to rush this experience. Take your time....

When you are genuinely feeling a definite emotion surrounding this event, discover what it is—name it. Is it fear? Is it anger? Is it guilt or shame? Whatever emotion your child within is feeling, allow it to come to the surface. You have every right to feel *all* your emotions. If this emotion is one which you no longer need to hold onto, begin releasing it now. Tell the other person(s) in your picture window scene that you no longer want to feel this emotion and you are letting it go. You no longer need to feel anger, fear, guilt, or shame. Release it!

Now slowly, begin to re-create the event you have witnessed through the window. Allow your child within to tell and show you just how they would have liked the event to unfold. Imagine that exact situation unfolding before your eyes. Re-create the emotions you no longer wish to hold onto by re-creating the very experience which instigated them. After this re-creation is complete, hug your child within and walk hand-in-hand through the imaginary picture window and back into your present reality.

Child Within Journal

Child Within Journal

9 For-Giving

> ˙Old hurts cannot be cancelled and undone, but these emotions can become the seeds of transcendence that allow healing to occur, whether we are the victim or the aggressor.
>
> —Joan Borysenko

You have recognized your hurt and woundedness from the past, thus seeking a way to mend and heal it. You have recognized the emotions attached to your pain and learned ways to release them. You have learned how to re-create your past, to re-experience it in a more positive manner. All the processing you have completed up to this point in your recovery has directed you to the act of for-giving.

What does "forgiveness" mean to you? I asked several people what their definition of forgiveness was and received various answers. Many thought forgiveness meant to let go of the past; others said it was a feeling of getting in touch with the Divine. I believe it is important to understand that the word "for-giving" is a *verb,* meaning "to give." It is an *action* you choose to do. The person who wants to begin forgiving assumes the action. The receiver of this act need not do anything, or even know they are being forgiven.

Giving is the action which takes place in the process of for-giving. You give to yourself and to others. You give yourself the *freedom* to be all you are *becoming.* You acknowledge and give yourself the "power of choice" to be free from guilt, victimhood, fear, or any emotion which is inhibiting your total expression as an adult. You accept yourself as you are. You forgive yourself.

You give others *their* freedom to be who *they are becoming.* You acknowledge them for who they are—faults, fears, emotions, neuroses and all. You give others the freedom *to be at the level of awareness which they are presently.* Even though you may not agree with everything your offenders represent or the actions they have taken, you give them the choice to live their life as they choose. You accept others as you desire to be accepted. You forgive others and allow them their journey of *becoming.*

The act of forgiveness is a *conscious choice.* You are in control of the process. No one can force you to forgive yourself or others. Forgiveness requires a certain level of human compassion and spiritual enlightenment. It is an act of *self-empowerment* which only you can perform. Self-empowerment marks the ability to accept and own your personal power. Self-empowerment occurs when you no longer allow others to impact your reality negatively. For-giving allows you to claim this power and accept the responsibility for your emotional reactions.

There are four stages in the for-giving process:

1. To recognize your hurt and the emotions it generates.

2. To acknowledge who you are at this moment and accept yourself fully.

3. To acknowledge others for who they are and accept them on a spiritual level.

4. To employ the "power of choice" not to hurt, or be hurt, in the same manner.

You have already completed the first stage in for-giving. You have acknowledged that you were wounded as a child. You have recognized your hurt and trauma. You have also discovered the different emotions attached to your woundedness and begun processing, releasing, and re-creating them into more acceptable feelings. However, you may still be carrying your hurt with you like a piece of weighted baggage. Do you keep guilt, shame, victimhood, fear, anger, or hate alive by allowing it to control your actions and reactions? The next stage in for-giving will help you to fully acknowledge who you are, accept yourself, and move into self-forgiveness.

Facing and For-Giving Yourself

To forgive yourself requires facing yourself—warts and all! Can you confront your own emotions and patterns? Can you squarely face what goes on *inside*? These questions addresses the possibility that many times we do not clearly see our own faults, foibles, and neuroses but instead project them onto others. To for-give yourself requires total conscious awareness of who you are, in the present. In the Chapter "Mirror, Mirror on the Wall," I suggested that your personal reflection can be clouded with a "fog-like" mist which restricts and hides your true-Self. This mist hides positive personality traits as was previously discussed, but more importantly, it can hide self-defeating traits and patterns as well.

If you have completed some of the exercises within this book, you may feel you have successfully re-created your past emotions and woundedness. Study yourself even closer for the tiniest sign that you might be holding onto deeper emotional aspects from the past which are blocking your total self-acceptance. Examine yourself thoroughly to check if you demonstrate fear in any form. Explore yourself for signs of dislike, disgust, or apathy toward yourself. Check for and acknowledge your foibles, faults, and failings. To forgive yourself requires learning who you are one hundred percent.

If you find hidden aspects of your pain which you have kept alive, now is the time to re-create them and let them go. How do you accomplish this task? By completely loving who you are right now this very moment. Turn to your true-Self and feel the empowerment of knowing you are special. You are a Light which no one can extinguish. Accept yourself as you are today, a loving, caring human being with much to express. When you arrive at the total realization of who you are, this minute, and truly accept that image, you are on your way to self-forgiveness.

Many times, one experiences self-dislike as a fear, a hallucinatory monster or "being," or a part of themselves which they "cannot stand" within themselves. This self-doubt and self-hate can enter and disrupt all stages of life. It can influence the choices one makes, the actions taken, and the kinds of relationships encountered. If you have experienced any of these aspects or just a "bad feeling" about yourself because of your childhood experiences, take a moment to get in touch with this sense of self-destruction. Go into a light autohypnosis and see the fear, the monster, or the being clearly in your mind. See yourself slowly approaching it and peel its mask right off. Most often, an insight or an answer is uncovered which shows you why you have been afraid to share yourself completely, why you dislike or doubt yourself.

One client, after completing the above exercise, shared that she found her own child within behind the mask. She uncovered how she had been hating herself for years because of her childhood experiences. Another client peeled back the mask of her fearsome dragon to reveal her mother's face. This indicated to her that she had not completely processed through her fear regarding her mother's over-protectiveness during childhood.

Are you facing what is actually going on inside yourself? This same question asks if one can observe oneself in the "moment" without benefit of past memories or hurts. To truly face oneself in the moment, you must let go of the past and move forward into the present. Spiritual teacher Krishnamurti defined the word "experience" as an event "to go through." This denotes that one go through an experience to the finish point, not to retain it but to perceive it only in that moment. However, we do retain our experiences through our memory and our emotions. If you try to experience an event in the present without retaining it in some fashion, it becomes impossible.

We live in the past in many ways. If someone says something to you which "hurts your feelings," you retain that emotion in the form of a memory of that person and experience. When you meet that person again, your memory responds with the hurt and painful emotions you experienced. It is impossible to say something cruel or act violently towards another without it leaving its mark. Krishnamurti related, "One has been hurt and one lives in that consciously or unconsciously," meaning the past is either unconsciously retained and repressed or the memory stays n our conscious recall.

You can begin to live in the present by releasing the retained hurt and not allowing it to direct your life. You can accomplish this by using self-empowerment, by acknowledging your personal power. When you "retain a past hurt in your brain" (consciousness) and incorporate it into your current decisions and actions, you are living with echoes of powerlessness. You are actually giving up your power to the person who hurt you!

At this point in your healing, you may feel you have completely rid yourself of the negative past. If, however, you have retained the memory of your childhood experiences by clinging to the emotions of fear, self-doubt, victimhood, anger, guilt, or shame, you are passing your personal power to another, whether they are living or dead. These emotions inhibit your thoughts, actions, reactions, and choices. The remnants of your past hurt and trauma can even lead you to self-destructive behaviors and blur your perception of yourself and others.

One young woman found after studying herself more closely that she had kept herself from finding a genuine, honest, caring relationship for many years because she had not forgiven herself for her earlier divorce. She had chosen very abruptly to end her first marriage while in her twenties after only a few years and felt she had let go of that part of her life. However, upon closer examination, she found a remnant of guilt remaining about her decision to end her marriage. This hidden guilt was inhibiting her from dating and being social with men. She, in fact, came to realize that her unconscious guilt was actually stopping her from finding another suitable relationship. Once this was realized, she took her first conscious steps toward forgiving herself for the decision to divorce her husband. She is no longer bound by past guilt. She is choosing to live actively in the present.

Now is the moment to let go of any leftover self-destructive patterns. It is the time to recognize and release "the memory of hurts" which can become a self-destructive pattern like negative habits, addictions, anger flare-ups, fear motivated behavior, controlling guilt or shame, non-communicative treatments, isolation and loneliness, passive-aggressive traits, or any other form of self-undermining. For-give yourself by freeing yourself from restrictive patterns which hide your true-Self. Give yourself the freedom to be who you are becoming. *Self-forgiveness occurs when you no longer give power to your hurt.*

Facing and For-Giving Others

If the word "forgiveness" gets stuck in your throat, you are not alone. Many people find it difficult to totally forgive those who hurt them when they were a child. If you find yourself hesitant at this point to proceed with the for-giving process, let me share my feelings regarding forgiving others. You, as an adult, can easily learn to forgive others by using the stages listed in the beginning of this Chapter—recognizing the hurt, facing and acknowledging yourself and others, letting go of the past and its hold on you, and making sure not to hurt or be hurt again in the same manner. However, your "child within" may not have the capacity to follow through with these stages. There may always be a small part inside of you which cannot forgive, this part is the child inside which actually experienced the hurt.

The child within, which is till so much a part of each of us, does not have the developmental ability to consciously forgive those who hurt him or her. The child within merely remembers the pain and hurt and may not have the reasoning ability to initiate the act of forgiving. To forgive another, one must possess the understanding, compassionate mind, and the spiritual unfolding of an adult. For this reason, many people have not been able to forgive their attackers; they are not working from their adult perceptive. These people are bound to the past because they have allowed their inner child to control their emotions, actions, and reactions. You can liberate the child within's control by moving into the adult you are today; then you will fully reap the effects which accompany forgiveness.

Can you face others without the past—without all the accumulated memories, insults, and hurts—and see them through clear eyes? Krishnamurti stated: "One, I have been hurt and that creates a great deal of neurotic activity, resistance, self-protection, fear; all that is involved in the past hurt. Second, how not to be hurt any more." The first step is to acknowledge and let go of the resistances and self-protection patterns adopted in childhood which are still being employed. These are the maneuvers you used as a child to survive trauma, they are no longer needed in adulthood. Once you face the many different types of camouflage you possess and then let them go, you begin the process of self-forgiveness. You begin to see yourself clearly. Then you can approach the task of seeing others through clear eyes.

How do you accomplish seeing your attackers (the persons who hurt you) with clear eyes? You face them within yourself; they have made their mark there. You may have built a wall around a particular hurt, withdrawn from life in some manner, but you always react from that center of hurt. Therefore, you are acting from fear—fear of being hurt in the same manner. This type of reaction keeps you living in the past, hanging onto old baggage. It also drains your sense of personal power. It is time to face your fears and face your offenders. You do not need to literally confront your parents, siblings, or the others who hurt you; or, you may wish to do so. What *is* important is to face them clearly and see them for who they are—*their* warts and all!

One way to begin clearly seeing another person is to know their history. If you have the time and inclination to research the background of those who hurt you, you may find quite an interesting story. Many of my clients were amazed at the details they uncovered about their father, mother, and other relatives while researching their family of origin. The image of these people which they had carried with them for many years changed before their eyes. This exercise can be most revealing. Remember, an image is just that, *an image*. It can change in a flash of insight.

We all live in our own psychological prison. We have sets of images for everything in our reality. We perceive ourselves and our world within an image; we form pictures in our minds of how we appear to others; we imagine our goals and dreams; we have created an image of ourselves and our reality which aligns with our perception of who we are. To change an image of someone which has haunted us with past trauma sounds difficult. It is not, it only requires seeing the image in a new Light.

Now that you have begun processing your past painful experiences and emotions and have learned how to face and forgive yourself, you can learn how to re-create and let go of images and feelings about others which are draining your power. Be assured that you may not want to forgive many of the "actions" taken by those who hurt you. Many actions or behaviors could never be accepted or condoned. The *action* may never be forgiven, however, the *person* may be.

Holding onto an old image of your offender keeps you locked into a pattern of restriction and self-limitation. It is important to develop a path of spiritual understanding which permits you to move forward. You begin this journey right where you are, acknowledging and seeing others for who they are and ultimately re-creating your hatred, judgment, and blame into images of awareness, acceptance, and for-giving. Coming from this new perspective, you can literally change embedded images of others, see your perpetrators in a new light, thus giving yourself the gift of self-empowerment. *Forgiveness naturally occurs when you no longer give your power away.*

Acknowledging your offenders for who they are on a physical level is easy. Seeing someone physically as a bully, brut, or manipulator is not difficult. Look deeper, beyond the physical and into their soul, search for their very spirit. I believe in the philosophy of Oneness and the unity of All. Within this belief is the concept that we are all part of the same Whole. If you want to find duality in your world, humankind has made it easy—the body and the mind, spirit and matter, good and evil. However, there are no dualities, only illusions, images of the Divine force in constant creation. When you can bring this concept into your reality you will experience a great shift in your attitude toward others and for-giving begins.

Remember Bruce and his criticizing father? When Bruce acknowledged his anger toward his father, he did not believe he could ever forgive him. However, after a few months of soul-searching and facing his old image of his father, Bruce decided to telephone him. He was surprised to find a different person at the other end of the telephone. He heard a calm, gentle person, one he had not imagined. As he began to talk with his father as an *adult,* not allowing his child within to interrupt his conscious awareness, Bruce learned of many new aspects about his father which he had never guessed. He listened to his father tell of his own bruised childhood and began to understand and see him more clearly as a person, not just a father. After their conversation, Bruce's pain and anger lessened. He related that he felt more compassion for his father and could forgive him "just enough" to see him in a new perspective, a new Light.

Bruce forgave his father *just enough* to ensure his peace of mind. How much forgiveness is "enough?" The choice is yours. You may find a very small amount of forgiveness is possible in some situations with some people; with others, a total giving of acceptance for who and where a person is on their life's path may be permissible to you. The question of how much forgiveness is enough reminds me of another question I read in Timothy Ward's book *What the Buddha Never Taught,* it went something like this:

> "How big is a stick?" the guru once asked his disciples. One bright learner responded proudly, "It depends on what you want to use it for, doesn't it? If you need a bigger one, then it's too small. If you need a smaller one, then it's too big. A stick isn't big or small at all. It becomes so as a product of your desires."

How much for-giving is enough? As much as is necessary to get the job done. Do not be concerned with the amount of forgiveness you have to offer; the quantity is not as important as the quality. A small silent voice can resound forever.

The Power Of Choice

Did you feel unsafe as a child? Do you feel safe as an adult? If you answered "yes" to both of these questions, you are no doubt preventing yourself from being hurt in the same manner you were as a child. However, if you answered "no" to the second question, you may be setting yourself up for more of the same type of hurt and pain. As children, we learn about safety first hand. We learn quickly which kinds of behaviors are acceptable in our family and which are to be avoided. We learn what makes us feel safe and what threatens that safety.

To complete the final stage of "for-giving" you must be *in control* of your safety. As a child, many times we could not control our own safety, but as an adult, *you* possess that control. That control is called your "power of choice." If you are living in a situation where you feel unsafe, perhaps now is the time to re-evaluate it. In childhood, at a very young age, we are conditioned to respond to our parents and others in particular ways. We learned to give up our own power of choice and many times our safety. As an adult, we can take back our personal power and "choose" where and how we want to live our lives within the imperative feelings of personal safety.

No doubt you vowed that you would never let anyone ever hurt you again like you were hurt as a child. You formed an image of yourself surrounding the type of hurt you felt and swore you would never let that happen to you again. This is one way of feeling and taking your power back. However, this route directly deals with past trauma by "retaining the past experience" instead of letting it go and living in the present without the fear of having your safety threatened. This method of trying to take back your power actually operates from the center of hurt itself. Instead of manipulating your image of pain by trying to defensively "ward-off" more hurt, you can choose a completely new image of what living in safety means to you.

While working with this book, you have discovered many new ideas and techniques which have provided you with the means to re-create your self-image and your painful past. Allow this new image to outshine the old restricted picture of hurt and pain of an unsafe past. You no longer need to be afraid to use your own personal power to feel safe in your environment. Use your "power of choice" to begin living within the limits of safety which you deserve.

Is it possible never to be hurt again? Perhaps not, however, we *can* prevent ourselves from experiencing the same type of hurt from the same people that we experienced in the past. If we keep allowing ourselves to be hurt in the same manner over and over again, we find ourselves wrapped in victimhood. We must allow our new image of self-empowerment and self-safety to lead us out of the victim role and towards a vision of compassion and for-giving.

My father had always proclaimed he was an atheist (someone who does not believe in a Higher Power) until he entered an alcohol rehabilitation and recovery program. His spiritual unfolding was such a pleasure to witness. Alcoholics Anonymous was too public for him, however, he found his spirituality through other means. He discovered there are many paths to the top of the mountain.

When he finally realized and admitted he was an alcoholic and stopped drinking, his entire attitude toward himself and life in general changed dramatically. Once during this period, he told me with tears in his eyes that he was sorry for the times he had "rebuffed" me as a child. I cried too and at that moment I totally opened my heart to him; forgiveness came in a spiritual instant. I met my *real father* then while sitting on the edge of the bed in the rehabilitation hospital. We shared stories of our different perceptions of one another and learned we both were very special people.

In those shared moments with my father, I realized a sense of personal power which I had never recognized within our relationship. I acknowledged and accepted my own strength in our relationship and used my "power of choice" to let go of the *power-over feelings* which I had felt he possessed. During the next twelve years of sober living which my father chose to live, we became closer and more accepting of each other than I had ever dreamed possible. He could no longer hurt my old self-image for it no longer existed. I had learned to accept my own personal power, therefore, creating a new image of self-empowerment. In this manner, my father and I began re-learning and re-creating our relationship on an adult level. *Forgiveness occurred when I no longer gave power to my hurt or to those who hurt me.*

The connection between spiritual emergence and the act of for-giving is a profound one. Earlier, I commented that forgiveness requires a certain level of human compassion and spiritual enlightenment. Spiritual awareness can emerge in many shapes and forms. I believe one is not required to "submit" to a Higher Power in order to recover from wound-edness or addiction. One only need *seek and acknowledge* the spiritual nature within to reap its gifts of inner direction and healing. When the emergence of spiritual awareness (the transpersonal) combines with human compassion, the stage is set for the act of for-giving. One need not submit anything, only receive.

(You may not be able, or desire to have a one-on-one con-frontation such as Bruce or I encountered in our for-giving process, however, you can use the re-creation Exercises and the following Child Within Autohypnosis to guide you to a for-giving experience.)

Child Within Exercises

1. You have fully explored your present self-image. To help you fully acknowledge who you are in the present, write a short paragraph about who you believe yourself to be as an adult. (Do not read any further until completing your paragraph.)

Scale that paragraph down to one sentence. (Complete your sentence before reading further.)

Now, take that sentence and sum-up your current self-image in "one word."

Are you pleased with the word which remained to describe your image? If not, begin the second part of this exercise which is to start with a completely different word than the one above, a word which *positively* describes yourself. Then write one sentence to help elaborate upon that word and the image you desire to have about yourself. Finally, take the new sentence and write an entire new paragraph which reveals the new self-image you are re-creating for yourself.

Upon completion of this entire exercise, your self-image can be re-created into a positive, free, loving adult. Take this new image and live it out physically, mentally, emotionally, and spiritually. This is a big step in for-giving yourself.

2. Rituals of any kind are important in marking steps of progress within a span of time. Try another ritual to help you let go of old images and hurts. Go to a favorite nature spot and meditate in silence. Watch the clouds as they build in momentum and then travel on toward other destinations or dissolve completely. Let your mind and your pain travel with the clouds high above into the next level of being. Sit quietly for a period of time and consider your new self-image without hurt and pain. Can you also change the image you hold of those who hurt you?

You may wish to complete a ritual such as burying a stone, crystal, leaf, or shell to signify your letting go and moving on to for-giving. Perhaps a sound ritual of chanting, singing, or humming would help re-create your woundedness into for-giving. A fire ritual of burning incense, candles, letters, or childhood mementos can also help to bring you into the realm of letting go and forgiveness. Most of all, be in peace during your ritual ceremony, listen to the sound of your own smile and touch the depths of peace.

3. You have learned how to re-create emotions which were attached to painful childhood experiences. You can also learn to re-create into forgiveness an undesired emotion which still haunts you. While you were reading this Chapter, you may have uncovered a hidden feeling such as anger or hatred toward yourself or those who hurt you. The following exercise demonstrates how easily such emotions can be re-created.

Ask a trusted friend to read this exercise to you as you experience it, or, you may read it through then follow the instructions. Sit in a chair, close your eyes, and put your hands out in front of you face up resting on your thighs. Allow yourself enough time to settle into a light autohypnosis before proceeding.

> Sense your unwanted emotion and within your mind form it into the shape of a small square. See this square as dark brown or black in color, it may be full or empty. It smells like forgotten garbage and feels very heavy in weight. There is a loud deep rattling sound coming from it which is very disturbing to the ears. Now in your mind, place this square into your right hand. The weight of this emotion brings your hand down firmly on your thigh.

> Still with your eyes closed, see another object in your mind. This object may be round or cylinder-like in shape. It is light in color and may be full or empty. This emotion is compassion and it smells like sweet roses. It feels very light in weight and almost floats into your open left hand. There is a soft lovely sound being emitted from this ball which makes you want to hum silently to yourself.

> You can see, smell, and feel the distinct differences between these two emotions. Now very slowly watch the heavy dark square begin to lighten in color as it sits beside the round shape. Feel the square's weight gently start to lighten and the sound coming

from it begin to soften. At the same time, the round object is starting to become more solid and is changing in color. The square is now much lighter with a touch of sweetness coming from one corner. The loud noise is now the same humming sound as the round object in your left hand and can be heard easily. The round object has now become a bit heavier as the square becomes lighter still. The square has begun to change shape by forming more rounded corners. The rotten smell is now completely gone from it and the sweet smell of roses permeates both hands.

Watch as both objects form a new one with its own unique shape. The new object represents self-love, love for others, and inner peace. It is forgiveness.

4. Remember to take the stages of for-giving "one day at a time." No one is grading you on how well you forgive yourself or others. This is *your* healing and recovery journey, take it at your own pace. Take a moment to ask yourself questions like, "How would it feel to forgive myself? Would I change my living patterns if I totally accepted and forgave myself? How would others view me?" Also, ask yourself questions such as, "What would it feel like to actually forgive my offender(s)? How would I change? How would they change? Would it be possible for me to begin for-giving?" You may find writing your questions and answers in your Journal will help you make these first attempts at forgiveness easier.

If trusting others has been an issue for you over the years because of being hurt, make an effort to make new friends. Choose with who *you* want to share your time. Let yourself learn how to be a trusting friend and enjoy the rewards of a new relationship. Make mental notes to yourself, or write in your Journal, which old patterns seem to surface surrounding trusting others. Watch for self-effacing behaviors and codependence. If you can master friendship, you can master for-giving.

5. Many people who have experienced trauma in their childhood are vivid dreamers, whether they remember their dreams or not. This is because the active subconscious mind

is always trying to impart messages and lessons to try to help you understand yourself and your pain more clearly. We know scientifically everyone dreams each night, however, not everyone remembers their dreams. You can employ the techniques of Re-Creation Therapy™ in your dream world. Through dream work, you can re-create a negative, fearful "bad dream" into a positive, loving, successful one.

When you realize you have had a negative or frightening dream and wish to re-create it, just re-close your eyes and relax back into the dream keeping your same body position. Then let your mind visualize a re-creation of the dream like you would have wanted it to have happened. For instance, one re-occurring dream a client was experiencing was a scene of herself being lost in an open field. She could not see or hear anyone and felt abandoned, cold, and afraid. Each time she dreamed this dream she became more and more terrified of being left with no one to care for her. She began to re-create her dream into having many friends and relatives around her and feeling loved by them all. It took her only a few re-creation dream sessions to completely rid herself of the "abandonment dream" to feel secure within herself and not to fear being alone.

Re-creating dreams can be one of the best methods to work with your subconscious mind in re-directing your past emotions. When a negative feeling arises within a dream and you wake up, re-create that emotion along with the dream to form a positive sequence of events creating happy feelings of joy and love. *You have control over your conscious dream re-creation, make it fun and enjoyable.* There are no limits to the amount or types of dream re-creations you can experience. A hint to help you "remember" your dreams so you can re-create them: Ask your *subconscious mind* upon retiring to help you remember any important dreams. In this way, you will program your subconscious to remember those dreams which may need to be re-created.

Child Within Affirmations

I accept myself for who I am right now.

I clearly see others for who they are in the present.

I do not judge or blame myself or others.

I allow my spiritual nature to develop within me.

I choose to make my life safe and protected.

I gain strength as I forgive myself and others.

Child Within Autohypnosis

Allow yourself to use the relaxation methods you have developed while working with your child within. Feel yourself relaxing into a light autohypnosis and allow your body to completely release all tension and anxiety. This journey into your own subconscious will take you to a place of peaceful rest. Become familiar with the scenery around you as you imagine your peaceful retreat. Whether a forest with deep lush colors of browns and greens or an ocean secluded between cliffs and sparkling blue water... be there Now.

As you are walking within your secret paradise, you come upon a small treasure. You pick this object up and feel its texture. Knowing you must keep this talisman near you, you put it in a pocket for safe keeping. Your body feels energetic as you skip along the pathway, perhaps singing to yourself. Soon you arrive at your destination, a large circle clearing. Sitting silently in the center of the clearing, you begin to reflect upon your childhood and the hurt you experienced. Suddenly you hear a faint cry of a child. Looking intently into the area beyond the circle, you spy a small child standing alone. You motion the child closer and he/she approaches you silently. It is your child within.

Instructing your child within to sit beside you, it obeys. Non-questioning, the child begins to hum the tune you were beginning to sing. The two of you continue humming the tune feeling the closeness between you. At this time, allow your child within to give you the power to heal and forgive yourself. Allow your child within to give you the power to forgive others. You accept these gifts from your child within. You accept the ability to move out of the past and into the present.

Reaching down into your pocket you withdraw the small object from its hiding place and offer it to the child. Accepting your gift, the child hugs your neck and smiles with the understanding that precious gifts have been exchanged between you. When you feel completed with this meeting allow your child within to return to the outer edge of the clearing and out of sight. Feel your inner spirit filled with love and peace.

You are for-giving yourself and you are for-giving others at this very moment. You have become the free adult ready to begin a complete recovery.

Child Within Journal

Child Within Journal

Part IV

Gifts From
The Child Within

There comes a turning point when you look around and say,
"I really might be alright."
At that moment the doors open and life moves in.
—Emmanuel

10   Faces of Recovery

> The real is only one manifestation of the possible.
> —Ilya Prigogine

Can the above quote be true? You have proved it is. You have learned it is possible to pick and choose that which you wish to manifest. Take a moment to think of your life as a huge CD player. All your thoughts, emotions, experiences, values and beliefs up to this point in your life are etched on thousands of CDs from prenatal to present. Of course, you would not be able to remember all these events and emotions consciously, but just suppose you did. These thousands of CDs, then, would contain every act, thought, intuition, feeling, and so on, of your entire life. They would be the manifestation of your life.

Now envision if you will, one thought or belief in which you decided sometime in your life to change. This might have been a lesson in growing up, such as when you decided as a teenager that your parents were not always right; or perhaps, as an adult an emotion or belief was changed regarding a particular group of people because of an event or impression you witnessed. The changes you implement in the course of your life keep redefining *your reality*. You continually choose what your real life is by re-creating the past. You create yet another "possible" manifestation of your world each time you implement a change. The new reality is real, the CDs are real, and you have the choice to play the same ones over and over or select a new album altogether.

"The real is only one manifestation of the possible." You have learned how the process of Re-Creation Therapy™ validates this statement. You have recognized old belief systems, patterns, and emotions as only one manifestation of your possible reality. These old CDs, which have played for many years, have organized your experiences throughout your life for your perception was based upon them. They gave you justification for your actions and a device for remembering what was chosen in the past. However, now you have begun to *re-create your own reality*, thus manifesting new CDs containing unlimited possibilities.

Choosing to play a new CD from a new album is accomplished in the present. Remember the point of power is the present, not the past. Author Nancy Ashley said it clearly when she wrote, "We form our lives from our focal point in the present, at the point where our beliefs intersect with the physical world on the one hand and the non-manifest world on the other." Only in the present can you choose positive experiences to integrate into your life's CD player. You are creating and re-creating your reality each minute, you always have a choice to select a different CD.

You have clearly begun a personal recovery transformation by reading and working with the concepts and exercises within this book. This transformation may even be physically noticeable to you and others. Certainly, on an emotional level, you have undergone shifts and transformed undesired feelings and blockages into healthy attitudes. On the spiritual level, transformation may be more subtle and felt intuitively. In recounting your experiences with Re-Creation Therapy™, you can discern the stages of transformation which you have undergone. These stages are synonymous with any transformative process which results in a new idea, concept, or outcome.

Basically the four major stages of personal transformation found in Re-Creation Therapy™ are as follows:

1. An **awakening** desire to begin healing.

2. A **willingness to explore** conscious and subconscious memories.

3. An **integration** and reflection of the Gifts From The child within.

4. The formation of a personal **conspiracy** to begin re-creating your own reality.

(Adapted from "Stages of Transformation" by Marilyn Ferguson, 1980.)

The first stage of transformation began with an acknowledgement and investigation of your concerns about your life. This was an **awakening** to the possibilities of healing your past trauma. This entry-point became an inspiration to further your desire for recovery. Your awakening may have been triggered by new emotions, an emergent situation, or another's inquiry surrounding your life. Whatever or however your awakening desire to heal was first recognized, it became a vision of something better. An outlook of a brighter, more healthy way of living was awakened within you.

The next stage in your personal transformation was the **willingness to explore** your memories and emotions. This stage ensued when you took steps to reach for recovery by buying this workbook and sharing your childhood experiences by opening to your subconscious mind's storehouse of information and guidance. Exploring your inner most thoughts and fears by writing in a Journal; meditating and using autohypnosis exercises; and reaching into your childhood memories and touching your child within all account for the changes of perception you now retain of yourself and your reality. This willingness to explore was the onset of your personal transformation.

Thirdly, you learned to **integrate** the knowledge and mystery which you have uncovered into one clear, healthy picture of who you are becoming. The integration stage is one of reflection. It is a slow process of releasing the old and drawing-in the new. You may identify this stage of recovery as the stage you are in presently. It is the transforming stage of perfecting your beliefs, redefining and refining your goals, and testing your new concepts regarding yourself and your reality. In this stage, your thoughts are challenged with a new perspective and your desire to research and study different avenues of healing becomes paramount. Delving into metaphysics or other spiritual philosophies is common in this stage of personal transformation as well. Upon its completion, a synthesis is formed which reflects both the painful past and the freedom of the future. A new sureness of self and purpose is revealed which leads to a personal conspiracy to continue the recovery process.

The formation of this personal **conspiracy** is the final stage of your recovery transformation. It is recognized by a determination to let go of the past by re-creating it into a present filled with truth, self-love, and compassion for others. This stage marks the end of a life of victimhood and suffering and the beginning of a life filled with freedom and personal choice. At this stage, you see others in a new perspective, a new light. Their pain, or lack of it, becomes more visible. You may even find yourself using your new awareness and insight to assist others in their recovery process. A conspiracy to enable others joins the minds of all who seek *faces of recovery.*

Recovery at Last!

An obvious "shift in consciousness" occurs in the recovery process. A shift in consciousness to a new perspective, a new outlook toward your reality and ability to perceive it. There is evidence that we as a human race are entering a new paradigm of consciousness. Put more simply, this means our world is changing its view toward how we perceive ourselves in relation to others and the world at large. When such a shift in consciousness occurs on a personal level, one views a connected whole rather than the fragmented picture previously observed. The new picture contains every bit of information previously gathered and realized, and at the same time, it contains a new unified scope of reality.

To help you identify this concept in your own recovery, picture yourself in a small bedroom closet huddled in a corner in complete darkness. You place your hands tentatively out in front of you to touch the blackened space. At this point, your conscious reality is only an arm's reach, thoughts of restriction are not present. Now you place your hands beneath you and stretch them along the floor exploring the length and width of your reality of darkness. Your reality has expanded to include a foundation and a perceived space in which to grow, thoughts of restriction begin to form. Slowly you discover you can stand and move cautiously from side to side. This space of consciousness reveals the awareness of the possibility of Something More—Something Infinite.

At this moment, someone enters the bedroom, turns on the overhead light and opens the closet door. At first you may be blinded by the Light, then you quickly adjust your vision and begin to perceive your previously limited reality. Then you discover how your attempts to envision your reality had been restricted to mere fragments of the possible whole. This "shift in consciousness" awakens a new ideal (paradigm) within you. This shift brings with it an opportunity to heal the wounded perception you hold of yourself and begin recovery.

It does not need to take five, ten, or twenty years to accomplish your recovery from childhood woundedness. Each transformative stage takes only as much time as necessary for you to feel secure that you are ready to move on to the next. For some this may mean several years, for others just a few months. Trust your own child within and transpersonal-Self to guide you through each step. How will you know when you have succeeded in your transformation through recovery? The first difference you will notice is a new found sense of trust in yourself and others. This trust will seem to appear from out of nowhere and reflects a feeling of security within you.

Recovery will also be a feeling of accomplishment, of completing a process. Sometimes this feeling urges you to take on a whole new project such as seeking a career move or leaving an unhealthy relationship. At this stage, some people feel they can tackle any new task and quickly begin to explore new vistas, new areas of interest. There is a caution not to move too fast, allow yourself a little time to settle into you new persona. At the same time, do not hesitate to uncover novel ideas and new possibilities.

You will begin to recognize how free you are as a human being. The choices will pour in through many different avenues, explore them all! There are gifts in life, it is your turn to find them. At this time, you may realize you have the ability to *ask for what you want*. You are not afraid to stand up for your rights and desires and begin making healthy choices which lead to greater opportunities for growth. An intuitive glow of wellness shines from within you. The possibility of venturing into a spiritual philosophy may enter your mind at this time along with a sense of wholeness or a true knowing of that Something More.

Most often, negative patterns and habits and other undesired traits seem to be easier to control or alleviate all together at this stage in recovery. You are able to set limits when appropriate, and at the same time, be unlimited in your ability to reach out to unexplored territories. You begin to expand your knowledge and understanding to others. A true sense of compassion emerges with a sense of for-giving and you are able to love, laugh, and experience the joys of life while also conquering its sorrows. At this point, you know what it means to be a healthy, caring person who has arrived from a long healing journey ready to live in the present.

There are many who reach this final stage in the recovery process and find they have rid themselves not only of past emotional pain but also actual physical ailments. When a past wound festers and is not properly exposed to the healing elements of disclosure, nurturing and protection, it can deviate and infect other areas. But when the wound is recognized and tended to, a healing ensues on all levels.

Former Miss America of 1958, Marilyn Van Derbur, exposed her past wound of sexual abuse by her father from the age of five to eighteen years old. Marilyn shared her trauma of incest with America in the June 1991 issue of *People* magazine. She talked about developing acute anxiety with fits of sobbing and actual physical paralysis rendering her bedridden for long periods of time. Much of Marilyn's physical illness was later attributed to her childhood trauma. Her body had literally developed its own type of dis-ease at the same time she was desperately trying to keep her "secret" hidden. After years of various therapy treatments and the sharing of her sexual abuse, Marilyn is becoming the healthy, vibrant woman the nation envisioned her to be.

Many female incest survivors develop lower back pain, stomach disorders, severe constipation, or other physical symptoms of lower body distress in adult life which cannot be adequately diagnosed. After entering the healing and recovery stages of a transformative therapy, they report that the symptoms have diminished or disappeared. Other types of childhood abuse such as shaking, ear pulling, and head or face slapping can manifest in adulthood as severe migraine headaches, facial ticks, and ear infections.

Holistic health advocates believe we carry "cellular trauma" from childhood experiences of abuse into our adult years which may be dormant until triggered by an unknown stimulus. At different ages and with certain circumstances triggered, these cells surface to the conscious awareness in the form of pain and illness. In Marilyn's case when her own daughter turned five years old, the age she herself had begun experiencing sexual abuse, she manifested several real physical maladies. The connection between mind and body is so crucial it is important to recognize every symptom or illness which manifests in our body.

In my practice, I encounter clients with apparent healthy lives experiencing undue stress, anxiety, and undiagnosed physical discomfort. Without focusing on the physical complaints reported, together we explore their past childhood pain. Most often, after completing the third personal transformation stage (integration), these same clients share that their anxiety and other physical symptoms have greatly lessened or completely disappeared. *They transformed their physical pain by re-creating their painful past.* This is not to claim that all illness is related to childhood trauma, however, many have reported a direct correlation between the healing of their previous ailments and the healing of their child within.

We are just beginning to learn of the extraordinary connection between the human mind and body. The powerful physical signals our mind receives from our bodies, such as pain, are perhaps more acceptable to us than the power of our mind to control the physical body; however, we must not limit ourselves by believing we cannot use this wide resource of human mind power to help alleviate physical illness. As humanist and teacher Willis Harman once said, "Perhaps the only limits to the human mind are those we believe in."

Living in Recovery

For me, living in recovery has meant accepting my child within as a guide to my true feelings. I have always been the type of person that cannot get in touch with emotions at the drop of a hat. Many times in my life I have found myself in a situation I would rather not be in because I jumped in it before gathering all my emotions together. Too quickly I would think I felt a certain way only later to realize I acted out of loyalty, duty, or guilt. Now living in recovery, I allow my child within and my adult-self to take the time necessary to adjust to newly presented options. In this way, I am learning to examine all my feelings and the subsequent consequences before I act and/or react.

Living in recovery also has afforded me the opportunity to expand my goals and desires. I used to limit myself by thinking and projecting only within my comfort zone. For me, this was not allowing myself to imagine beyond the narrow reality of having children and mastering a new art/craft project every six months. Be assured, these experiences were fulfilling at the time for they were my childhood dreams, but I learned in the healing and recovery process to entertain much broader dreams for myself. I attended college, started a counseling career, and coauthored my first book *Beyond Words: A Lexicon of Metaphysical Thought.* By living freely in recovery, I was able to expand my dreams and goals with an unlimited mindset.

Also, living in recovery has inspired me to share this self-guiding therapy process which helped me to achieve peace of mind. However, with this sharing it was necessary for me to talk with my mother about disclosing the personal contents within this book. Previous to the book's publication, my mother knew about the abuse of her daughters as children; however, at seventy-six years old, it was a difficult reality to face again. Her strength and support at this time in my recovery has been greatly appreciated. Somehow deep within her, she realized this personal sharing would help others and this was her focus. It was painful for me to share the issue of my sexual abuse, but this final step closed the circle of my healing.

Living in recovery does not guarantee a painless existence, but the pain we encounter is acknowledged and dealt with on a new level. There is a sense of "cope-ability" added to our personal strength. In childhood we learned to survive, however, now we press forward to seek our truth. We let go of the past and its woundedness and find we have gained a present and a future. Take a few minutes at this time to write in your Journal what living in recovery means to you.

There is a story about a lighthearted monk who had strayed from the others and was leisurely walking down the mountain. Not knowing where to go next, he stops to look over the edge of a nearby cliff. He is so taken with the beauty of nature all around him that forgets he is lost and merrily begins to dance. His foot slips beneath him and he suddenly falls several feet over the cliff barely snatching an extending tree root which stops his fall into the canyon below. He is now hanging tenuously in midair as he notices there are two lions circling far below him. In studying this sight, he is so amazed by the lions' strength and prowess that he forgets he is near his fatality and begins to sing of the splendid animals. The tree branch he is holding onto begins to give way and he slips a bit further to what most would consider obvious destruction. Taking a moment to adjust himself, the monk spies a random patch of strawberries sprouting just inches from his face. Not hesitating for a minute, he seizes the moment to enjoy the taste of life.

This enlightening story illustrates how we can look life's traumas straight in the eye and still appreciate their treasures. Yes, we have admitted we were wounded in childhood, but we must also be willing to *live in our recovery* by acknowledging the pleasures and uniqueness of our world. Taking time to "taste the strawberries" is a conclusive way to speed the healing and recovery process. It is important in any recovery treatment to allow for spontaneity, laughter, and joy. *Self-discovery means not only exploring past woundedness, it means seeking to discover yourself living in the present.*

This "stop to smell the roses" philosophy allows you to seek newness in the life around you—to see a rainbow and taste its colors, to feel the touch of a single rain drop and hear the wings of a hummingbird. Take this time to enjoy your new found true-Self. Ralph Waldo Emerson wrote, "What lies behind us and what lies before us are tiny matters compared to what lies within us." It is this essence within which gives us the courage to look beyond our pain. It is this essence which can help bring playfulness and a sense of direction to our healing from past woundedness. And, it is this essence within us that stirs the magic ingredients for our recovery.

Child Within Exercises

1. Setting goals is an important part of any transformative process. As you enter the recovery stage of your healing, write down in your Journal your first impressions regarding new dreams to manifest. My initial list of new goals continued for several pages! I had no idea how many desires I actually had until I took the time to think about them and write them down. Once you have exhausted all your dreams on paper, check over your list a second time and put a "star" by each dream or goal you could begin to act upon. For example, if one of your goals was to find a new job and you felt you actually could start looking in the want-ads or calling a few friends for information, put a star by it. If on the other hand, one of your goals was to move to another state but your spouse could not leave his or her job location at this time, this goal might be set aside with no star by it for the time being.

Once you have thoroughly thought out each dream, each goal, and decided if you could act on a few in even the smallest of ways, pick **three** of these from your list. On a new piece of paper write these three dreams down, one below the other. Study each one carefully and get a feeling for which of these three goals you would feel comfortable beginning to act upon. Next to each word (or words) write what you would do first to start the process of attaining this dream or goal.

This initial action need not command your entire day, let it sit awhile until you feel completely comfortable with the thought of achieving it. Allow yourself the space and time to play with the idea of actually accomplishing this goal. Then act, take the first action necessary to start the project, select the tools, feel the success, and secure the aspiration. Accomplishing even the smallest of goals propels you through your transformation.

2. Challenge yourself to imagine you are living in recovery! Write or visualize exactly how you would be living if you were completely recovered from the pain of your childhood. What does living in recovery look like for you? How would you feel? Where would you live? Who would be sharing your

life with you? What kind of job or career would you be in? Would you be more healthy, wealthy, or wise? Let your imagination flow until you have completed a total picture of yourself living in recovery.

To help you visualize what living in recovery would be like, sense how your "future-self" would describe you to another person. Imagine you are ten years older than you are today, this is your future-self. Now, visualize what this future-self would tell his or her best friend about living in recovery from the age you are today. Listening to this conversation, hear the positive transformations which have transpired, sense the compassion and the happiness you have found. Envision your future-self talking about your freedom from past woundedness and victimhood. *Feel yourself actually living in recovery.*

3. Search through several magazines for dozens of pictures to cut out containing children of all ages that fit *your image of a happy child.* Find baby pictures, those of two year olds, pictures of preteens and some in adolescence. Now look for pictures of happy people in adulthood, cut out pictures of those in their younger years, through the middle years, and into the senior years. Put all these pictures on the table in front of you and begin to write "one" word on each picture that meets the feelings you want to attain once living in recovery. If you choose a picture of a rosy-cheeked infant with baby food all over his/her face, you might use the word "content" or "full." Use words that make you feel good, words that illustrate how you desire yourself to be.

After labeling all your pictures, begin pasting them randomly on a piece of cardboard. This is your personal collage of re-created ages of happy childhood and successful adult years—a reminder of your transformation. As you are pasting the pictures on the cardboard, let yourself feel your newly recreated Self as you let go of the past. Some of the pictures may overlap onto each other, let yourself play with where to place them. Now feel yourself transform into the vision of happy people you have chosen to represent yourself in recovery.

4. You may have already noticed the disappearance of minor aches and discomforts in your body as you have processed and worked with your child within over the past several months. Jot down these healing occurrences in your Journal. It is important to acknowledge, on all levels (body, mind, and spirit) the changes which you are undergoing as you experience the techniques of Re-Creation Therapy™. Have you noticed any changes? Do you feel more healthy, more centered? Are there any illnesses which seem to have disappeared? Once you have entered the recovery transformation stage of **integration**, watch the miracles of healing begin.

5. For many, growing up is most often a painful process. From our earliest childhood, we reach for the goal of being a "grownup" only to find it beyond our reach. During a lecture many years ago, author Marilyn Ferguson commented that the word grownup "...really means grown-dead. When we tell a child or ourselves to grow up, we mean get serious, don't play, don't laugh, don't get excited." When we shut down all these spontaneous childlike qualities, emotions such as anger, frustration, guilt, and fear begin to surface. Grownup and grown-dead mean the same thing if you suppress your spark of inner child-like qualities.

Just as the monk took the time to taste the strawberries of life, allow yourself to listen to the music of a waterfall. Hike on a path in the mountains and hear the leaves rustle beneath your feet. Swim in a lake or the ocean's blue-green waves and let the sun dance on your shoulders. In your recovery there is a myriad of activities waiting to be experienced for the first time, or perhaps more accurately "acknowledged" for the first time. Living in recovery means letting go of the past and seizing each day and filling it with treasures to remember. Your child within can bring you these gifts if you but allow yourself to receive them.

Child Within Affirmations

I am undergoing a recovery transformation.

Each day I experience a treasure.

My essence is pure and directs me to total recovery.

I enjoy each day and seek out new experiences.

My recovery from woundedness is complete and I let go of the past.

I accept the gifts from my Child Within.

Child Within Autohypnosis

Lie down on your back with your arms at your sides, put a small pillow beneath your knees and one under your head. Close your eyes gently and begin to relax. Take several deep breaths through your nose expanding the abdomen area then release the air out through your mouth as your stomach descends. Allow yourself to more completely relax with each new breath, releasing tension and tightness. Tell each of your body parts to go limp and soft. Starting with your head, release all muscles, smooth lines, relax the back of your neck. Tell your shoulders to relax then carry that relaxation down through your upper body, down your legs and into your feet.

Once totally relaxed, take one last deep breath and exhale out any remnants of anxiety. Feel your arms lying heavily and motionless at your sides and feel the deadweight of your thighs and legs. You are totally relaxed and ready to begin counting down in your mind from your present adult age ....60, 59... 50, 49... 41, 40... Slowly count downward one year at a time. As you do this, some scenes from past years may appear in your mind's eye; release them as you continue to count yourself down into your teenage years. When you arrive at an appropriate age in your teen years, you will automatically stop. Let your mind filter through the pictures of yourself at this age that are important to your recovery. Gently hug this adolescent child within and ask him/her to follow you as you once again begin to count downward into your preteen years.

Let yourself be guided to stop at an age between eight and twelve years old. When you have met your child within at the age chosen, allow him/her to hold you and follow you and your adolescent as you count down to an even younger child within. Stop to meet your child within between the ages of two and seven years old. Let him/her also get close to you to convey affection and caring. At this point, you may wish to include another age of your child within to accompany you and the others. See each chosen child within clearly and ask them all to follow you to meet your infant-self. Count down to an early age just months after your birth, your infant. Hold in your arms the infant you once were and ask all the others to follow as you walk to your special place of peace.

Once you and all your chosen child within ages arrive at this place of silence and security, form a complete circle. You are still holding your infant-self, your adolescent child within is standing beside you and the others are completing the circle. Gently place the infant on a pillow in the center of the circle and look into his/her clear, shining eyes. Tell each of the others to look into these eyes, the eyes of their own innocence, and allow them a few minutes to make this loving connection. The infant knowingly smiles back at each of the children chosen to represent his/her life with a true sense of compassion. This link allows each inner child to feel the pure love they too possess within their hearts.

Now join hands with this family circle and ask each inner child if they would like to say a few words about their ability to live in recovery through you, the adult. Let each child within express itself to you by telling you how they can let go of their hurt and allow "you" to move on into recovery. Take as much time as necessary to complete this emotional link with your family within.

When each inner child has completed his/her sharing of support for your release of woundedness and living in recovery, take each one by the hand and hold them gently explaining you will always be available for them. They may offer a few last words or gifts, accept them with an open heart. Then leave your family circle as they stand together supporting one another in this place of peace.

Slowly begin to count yourself up from infant to one year, two, three, four, and so forth into your adult years, 30, 31... 40, 41.... until you once again reach your present age. As you count up to your present age, visualize yourself giving each of your adult-selves the gifts of love, freedom, for-giving, Light, courage, or other gifts you received from all your child within family circle. Feel the lightness of your body as you enter more consciousness and gently begin to move your toes and fingers. Remembering every word, every gift, every scene you experienced, open your eyes and begin *living in recovery.*

Child Within Journal

Child Within Journal

11 The Present and Beyond

> Often we only know we've been in a certain place
> when we pass beyond it.
> —Ram Dass

As you recall, the process of Re-Creation Therapy™ entails seven steps which guide you through self-discovery and self-recovery. The first step is acknowledgement: To acknowledge that there is a concern, a problem, a reason to seek healing. The second step is self-awareness: To fully understand who you are becoming and accept your total self. Third, meeting your child within: Learning that your true-Self is still within you, always with you, and ready to guide you with healing insight. The fourth step is releasing emotions: Using exercises and various techniques to direct your release of pent-up or repressed feelings surrounding your childhood suffering; to recognize and explore fear, anger, guilt and shame and release these saboteurs. Fifth is the actual Re-Creation: The re-creating of actual past painful experiences and the emotions attached to them into what you would have desired. The sixth step is for-giving: Actively forgiving yourself and others without judgment or feeling virtuous for this act. All of these steps have helped you reach your present point in recovery, no matter how long it has taken you to get here.

The seventh and last step in the Re-Creation Therapy™ process is letting go: Actively letting go of the past by choosing to move forward into the present and beyond. Letting go means moving into the present *without retaining the woundedness from the past.* It means to live your life forward while learning from the past. You did not survive your childhood pain just to be stuck in it forever. You survived it to learn how to let it go. A philosopher named Kierkegaard once wrote, "Life can only be understood backward, but it must be lived forward." It is time to choose to live in the present, to seek adulthood. It is time to let go of childhood patterns and pain. It is time to begin creating the future!

Some of you may remember the 1985 motion picture *Back to the Future* starring Michael J. Fox. In this movie, he portrayed a teenager living in the 1980s who was able to travel back in time to the 1950s where he *re-created the past therefore changing his present reality and redirecting his future.* Does this concept sound familiar? It should, that is exactly what you have been doing within Re-Creation Therapy™.

The first time I saw *Back to the Future* I was surprised and delighted to witness the representation of Re-Creation Therapy™ being presented on the screen. Many of my clients at that time also commented how the general concept of the movie paralleled the basics of the process of Re-Creation. I knew then that the foundational truth of this healing process had been an inspiration given to many. The truth being: When you re-create the past (literally or in a visualization of the mind) your present and subsequent future also changes.

If you have followed the exercises and autohypnosis visualizations within this book, you have changed your reality and your perceptions of who you are—your self-concept and the ability to choose your reality has broadened. You have re-created your past childhood experiences and the emotions attached to them. You have delved into the past, re-created it and therefore altered your attitudes, beliefs, and feelings. In this process, you are redirecting your future by the very nature of cause and effect. Once you re-create your past, you entertain change which alters your present reality, thus ultimately your future.

In all three episodes of *Back to the Future*, Michael J. Fox possessed a time-traveling machine in which to carry him to his desired year of destination. You too have a time-traveling machine, it is called your subconscious mind. You have learned to use your powerful mind to travel into your childhood years and re-create traumatic and painful experiences into more positive memories and emotions. Your child within has led you to those experiences which caused you pain so you both could re-create and heal each event, each emotion. At this point in your healing and recovery, you may well understand your life more fully by looking backward, "...but it must be lived forward." Now is the time to explore the last step in the process of Re-Creation Therapy™, letting go of the past and stepping back to the future.

Moving Into Adulthood

You may decide to continue to work with your child within by continuing to re-create your past childhood experiences. The choice to continue processing your childhood woundedness can enable you to enhance your understanding of yourself and your reality. You can always continue to seek guidance from your child within while allowing this inner part to be expressed through you. At the same time, it is important not to let your child within overshadow your adult-self. For years you have been consciously and unconsciously defining yourself and your reality by the pain you suffered as a child. Now is the time to let go of that childhood and move into the *present and beyond.*

You possess the ability to take this last step into adulthood. It requires only a little practice and cultivation to live as a free adult. Many believe we enter adulthood directly after adolescence, at the age of twenty-one. This assumption is incorrect. Adulthood is that state of mind when one can integrate their child within, adolescent, and post-adolescent experiences, dreams, goals, and spiritual direction into one synergistic persona. This integration can take an entire lifetime and some people never attain it. Becoming an adult does not "just happen" when you blow out twenty-one candles. It is a process.

We have been "becoming" adults our entire life. The true adult contains many components which form a complete autonomous individual who can share his or her knowledge and intelligence, love and compassion, fears and pain, and at the same time be able to receive these components and direct others who seek guidance with these determinants. Many feel their parents did not fill this definition of an adult, did yours?

It has been quoted that eighty percent of helping professionals are from dysfunctional families and that seventy-five percent of the clients who seek therapy have been affected by alcohol. Statistics such as these make it possible to comprehend just how our society has been crippled by childhood suffering and how many of our own childhoods were filled with pain and woundedness. It also becomes clear that our "adult" society is functioning under the guise of adulthood. These statistics tell us we did not grow up with the necessary adult parenting to ensure our own autonomous adulthood. They also point to our children's plight for becoming autonomous adults.

Becoming a free autonomous adult means letting go of many *safe* patterns of thinking and behaving we employed to survive the past. It means facing yourself squarely in the mirror and acknowledging who you really are and being willing to transform those aspects which you find lacking. It means letting go of past hurt in order to experience yourself openly, without judgment in the present. It means for-giving yourself and others, to reach beyond the present to challenge the future. You have accomplished many of these steps to becoming an autonomous adult by processing and re-creating your inner child's experiences and emotions through the exercises and autohypnosis visualizations.

The following list of characteristics may help you understand how an autonomous adult functions. Read down the list and circle the numbers for the characteristics you presently possess:

1. You *voluntarily* are responsible for your actions and reactions, emotions, and spiritual nature.

2. You are assertive, you have the ability to act, to have an impact on your reality; you have personal power.

3. You continue to expand your self-esteem with forward thinking; you choose what you want to do with your life and future while at the same time being able to consider others.

4. You have integrity at all times; you treat your reality as a partner in life; you have impeccable thoughts.

5. You trust yourself and your choices. You trust your intellect, your own judgment. You trust your intuition, your gut feelings. You trust your child within, your true-Self. You trust your emotions, what is right or wrong for you. You trust your body's signals by feeling the messages of stress—butterflies in the stomach, headaches, rapid heart beat, and so forth. You know when and whom to trust and you are trustworthy.

6. You set your own ideals and principles. Ideals of the *unseen* such as love, health, trust, right and wrong are clear for you. Your principles (boundaries) are also clear and strong, such as how far you will go to make your point. Your limitations regarding lying, trusting, wrong-doing, cheating, and hurting others is well defined.

7. You know how to have fun! You can enlist your spontaneous child within and curious adolescent to guide you to obtaining happiness and joy in your life.

The autonomous adult contains all of the above aspects, and others, to form the synergy necessary between the child within, adolescent, nurturing parent, and supportive ego which binds the adult persona. You may find that you meet the above components of adulthood, if not, the numbers not circled indicate the beginning steps to explore in becoming a free autonomous adult.

Letting go of the past to move into the present requires an active choice to release any negative input that dictates you cannot have the positive reality you desire. Many people still believe the old philosophy which states "you made your bed, now you must lie in it." These people truly believe they do not deserve to succeed in their life, that they have no choice but to follow their old path of suffering and hardship. You have the necessary tools to move beyond this type of negative outmoded patterning.

If you find yourself identifying with this type of powerless thinking, make a conscious choice right now to release it.

Write an affirmation of personal power in your Journal which allows you to let go of any negative ties with your ability to choose the present as you desire it to be. An example would be: I let go of restricting thoughts which limit my ability to move into the present. When you have decided on the wording of your affirmation, tape it to the mirror, refrigerator door, and inside the car. Take the *action* necessary to allow yourself the freedom to release any limitations which are holding you back from the present reality you desire.

Let Go – Let Child

There is a familiar maxim which affirms, "Let go, let God." This affirmation directs us to release our problems and worries to a Higher Power. It conveys to us that there is an inner core, a Divine essence, that can help us if we but let go and allow that part to direct our concerns. Your child within is also a part of that inner core, the true-Self which can guide you to your past and into the future. Allow yourself to let go and let your child within lead you to who you are becoming. You have processed through much of your childhood pain, now is the time to let go and reach for the present and beyond.

Let go of any inability to live as a healthy whole adult. An incapacity to let go may still root you to a familiar existence—let this part go. One client who had worked with her child within for many months continued to feel as if she did not deserve to live as a free adult. She could not visualize herself living a normal life without the bondage of childhood suffering. I instructed her to very slowly begin visualizing herself in her immediate future as a happy and peaceful person. Gradually, I asked her to visualize her future filled with excitement and a new outlook toward expressing her true-Self. She learned to take one step at a time by adding new positive aspects to her vision each time she visualized a healthy future. With support, this client was finally able to let go of her inability to begin living in recovery by learning to explore her future.

Another inability to move into recovery may be your resistance to viewing yourself with a positive self-image. If you are still resisting the fact that you are perfect and whole just as you are, re-read Chapter Five. It is time to let go of any opposition you may have that dictates you are something "less than perfect."

Inspect your forehead once again to check for leftover self-imposed labels which speak of self-doubt or uncertainty. Re-experience Exercise #2 in Chapter Five which asks you to list the labels you feel you have held onto in your life. Are there any residual labels to process? If so, take some time to explore where they came from and then let them go.

Allow yourself more time to regain your self-confidence and step fully into your newly re-created present-self. You can begin with a small project and see it through to its completion. Goethe wrote: *Whatever you can do, or dream you can, begin it... Boldness has genius, power and magic in it.* Touch this magic by committing yourself to finish a simple task, cleaning your bedroom closets or garage, or volunteering your service to an organization. You can also start feeling more self-confident by greeting your true-Self in the mirror each morning with a smile. Allow yourself to tap into your renewed sense of spiritual power uncovered by your child within. Use the Child Within Autohypnosis at the end of Chapter Five as many times as you wish as a guide to release any negative self-images which may be limiting your recovery process.

Let go of any traces of self-victimization which could be impeding you. Releasing hints of weakness, martyrdom, or victimhood can catapult you into your future. Enlist the direction of your child within once again to disclose any leftover feelings of self-victimization. Instruct yourself to "ask for what you want" and be aware of your needs. Your timely arrival into a present filled with confidence and strength is due. You can accept this gift from your child within by taking charge of your life and speaking up for yourself. You can let go of victimhood, you are a survivor.

Let go of any codependent propensities. Your future is filled with independence and freedom of choice. Letting go of codependence releases you from others. Letting go of codependence proclaims you honor yourself and your choices.

Letting go of codependence demonstrates your acceptance of being a man or woman with your own unique abilities. Letting go of codependence says, "I love myself, now I can love others." It is time to take back your personal power and fly away from the nest of codependence.

Let go of the residue of fear, anger, guilt, or shame surrounding your childhood. It takes far more energy and effort to sustain these emotions than it does to let them go. These emotional saboteurs can hold tight to your memories of trauma and suffering. If you still find yourself retaining any of these feelings after repeatedly re-creating your childhood experiences of woundedness, go back and re-experience the Child Within Autohypnosis at the end of Chapter Eight. Allow yourself to release any trailing emotions attached to your memories. Memories are but the wallpaper of the mind and can be removed and replaced. Your repressed or lingering emotions can also be released. Let go now of any remaining hostile or negative feelings which are obstructing your path to living in recovery.

Let go of persistent self-blame. Let go of blame directed toward others. You have processed through many experiences of your childhood which caused you pain. Can you let go of the self-blaming and blaming of others which these events initiated? Affirming that you have begun to re-create your reality and move into the present is all that is needed to rid yourself of the negative mindset of past blame. No amount of self-punishment is necessary to carry with you into your enlightened future. Let go of any remaining hints of blame for your past; it is time to voluntarily accept responsibility for creating your future. Allow your free adult to enter your awareness and liberate your child within from its confining blame. Give yourself permission to let go of blame and forgive yourself and others. Use your never-ending "power of choice" to begin your present and future with absolution.

As stated in the Introduction of this book, there is not a ribbon at the end of the race for recovery. It is an ongoing race. You have steadily processed your childhood woundedness by re-creating your past. You can begin to let go of that past by choosing one aspect at a time which may still be binding you and then release it. Choose one restricting thing, one emotion, one event, one attitude, one thought, one person to let go of forever. Take as much time as necessary to completely purge yourself of each destructive element which is preventing your recovery from growing up in a dysfunctional family. Continue to select one issue at a time to release until you are living in the present.

You have used your unique mind to touch the magic of your child within. In turn, you have re-created a new personal story. To complete your recovery process, take a few minutes to write down your feelings and the ways in which you have changed since employing the autohypnosis visualizations and other exercises found within this book. Review how you have progressed through your childhood pain to your present status of living in recovery by re-reading your notes and personal Journal. Become aware of the transformation you have undergone in letting go of a fragmented identity to re-create a reality filled with autonomy and freedom of choice. Be assured the efforts and discoveries you have already undergone will continue to enrich your life.

Allow yourself to feel the success of your healing. Celebrate your recovery with your child within by taking one minute of every hour to fill your thoughts with strength and self-love. There *is* a perfect life—and you and I are living it!

Parents of Adult Children

At the same time that we are working desperately to become adults, many of us are being confronted with the trials of our grown children who are also seeking adulthood. If you have grown children who are working through their own childhood woundedness and negative patterning, I offer a little insight and much support. My two children are processing and healing from their own dysfunctional family environment. My husband and I divorced when they were ten and twelve years old. We became one of the millions of American families who separated and caused pain to our children. Now that they are young adults, I am being presented with their questions, anger, and woundedness surrounding their childhood. This new element in my recovery dictates that as I continue to heal my childhood, I am also required to face the hurt I caused my own children.

Viewing myself through their eyes is enlightening and frightening. It is a joy to see traditions and values kept alive, and at the same time, difficult to openly acknowledge the limiting fears, negative patterning, and destructive behavior we passed down to them. This non-intentional generation to generation inheritance of verbal and nonverbal data becomes evident when viewing our children's habits, actions, and life choices.

An amusing story relating this truism begins with a newly wed couple attempting their first Thanksgiving dinner feast. The husband watches as his bride cuts off the ends of the juicy roast they are preparing and asks, "Honey, why do you cut the ends of the roast? Does it make it more flavorful?" The dutiful wife replies, "Well, I don't really know. It's just what Mom always did." This answer was not sufficient for the curious groom who wanted to get to the bottom of his query. He asks his bride to call her mother and ask the same puzzling question. The wife complies and asks her mother, "Mom, why do you always cut the ends off a roast before cooking it?" Her mother replies, "Because your grandmother always did." Now the husband was even more determined to get a satisfying answer, so he instructs his wife to call across the nation to ask her grandmother the same question! The answer they receive from the grandmother is quite unpredictable. She calmly reports, "Well, back in those days the roasting pots were so small I couldn't get a whole roast to fit into it so I cut off the ends." There was no secret cooking recipe or mysterious explanation to this traditional behavior. It had just become a nonverbal patterning behavior handed down from mother to daughter for generations.

Stories like this one can be found within every family, such as how to hang the roll of toilet paper, what kind of behavior takes place when company visits, or how the holidays are celebrated. Many family traditions are harmless and can even be enjoyable. However, when the behavior or expectation being handed-down is destructive, a closer inspection of the family tree may reveal some surprising roots. We know that if you were born into an alcoholic family background, you have a fifty percent greater chance of becoming an alcoholic. We also know that if one or both of your parents were abusive to you, you have a predisposition to abusing your own children. Statistics such as these can be prevented if we, as parents, process through our own childhood woundedness, therefore halting destructive repetitious patterning.

Someone once said *adults* undergo psychotherapy for their *kid's* sake. This could not be more accurate. Each of us must heal and recover from our own personal woundedness to successfully instruct and guide our children. When one of my children approaches me with a question regarding their childhood, I try to allow them their own feelings by not dismissing their emotions or questions or by painting a more pleasant picture than the truth. Although this response is not always easy, it is exactly what I would want from my own parents if I confronted them with my childhood history. It may be difficult to view our past behavior and choices through our children's eyes. What is important to remember is that any support and honesty we can give them at this point in their lives is well worth the effort, both for them and for us.

One of the greatest gifts we can give our grown children is a strong sense of personal choice. They must challenge us, their parents, and all that we stand for within their illusional reality. Just as we have needed to question our own upbringing, they are searching for their personal story in which we have played a big part. They may not yet relate to a sense of normalcy within their life—boundaries, values, and ideals may need to be explored. Many people raised in dysfunctional families require an abundance of reassurance of their being normal. It is important to share with them that we do not expect perfection from them and at the same time instill within them that they **are** perfect. We must remind ourselves to let go of our children to allow them to follow their own path with their own choices.

If you feel you need direction in dealing with your grown children's recovery process, search out a recovery support group. These nationwide groups can be a safe haven to find

both information and comfort from other parents being confronted with their children's healing and recovery. I have
found that sitting down and honestly answering my children's questions and sharing in their concerns has been the
opening door to our mending their past childhood wounds.

Listening to my children's memories of individual events
which took place in their (as well as my own) past is an eye-
opener. Their perception of many past experiences is far
more traumatic than my perception of the same incidents. It
is clear that what a child personally experiences is sharper,
more exact at that time than how adults presume it to be.
This insight may ring true for you if you have also shared
your childhood experiences with your parents. Your own
inner child's memories are clear and alive. When your children begin asking you questions as to why you acted or reacted the way you did during particular events in their
childhood, study if or how you passed-on to them any of the
same type of patterning you yourself received while growing
up. You may be surprised with your discoveries. With each
hurtful experience my children share, I recognize more of my
own childhood pain and patterning.

We *can* stop the future generational cycle of unfavorable
patterning which seems to have followed us from the beginning of time. You will know if you have succeeded when your
children begin making their own personal choices and *still*
ask for your advice! "There are only two lasting bequests we
can hope to give our children. One of these is roots, the other
wings." Let us present our children with the gifts from our
own child within; self-discovery and self-recovery, along with
the roots of affection and the freedom to fly.

Recovery Reflections

The quote at the beginning of this Chapter reflects the
feelings of many in recovery: Often we only know we have
been in a certain place when we pass beyond it. Reflecting
back on your recovery process can be invaluable, even if you
are only a few months into it. Each time I mentally review the
past several years through my own recovery, it becomes even
clearer that I continue to explore my feelings and re-create

my present reality to allow my true-Self to shine—a Self filled with forgiveness and strength. Knowing that I now have the tools and the power to choose how I want to live each day gives me a personal commitment for which to strive.

Yes, I am a survivor. Yes, I am in recovery. I acknowledge where I have been and I choose to "pass beyond it." Within you is the power to stand tall, let go of the past, claim your strength in the present and move beyond it into the future. By using the transpersonal counseling tools learned within this book and at the same time staying in tune with your own true-Self, you have all that is necessary to make appropriate decisions for your future. Connecting with this spiritual dimension of living is the key.

Recently, I heard one of my counseling mentor's state: "Spiritual disciplines teach us how to forgive others; psychotherapy teaches us how to forgive ourselves." This statement rang-true for me. It requires both an inward exploration of the self and a connection to the Self to journey through our lives with grace. The application of these two soul-searching practices can bring us peace to heal and move forward. This reflection by Vietnamese Buddhist Thich Nhat Hanh relates how we can simultaneously employ these avenues in our daily life:

> If a child smiles, if an adult smiles, that is very important. If in our daily life we can smile, if we can be peaceful and happy, not only we, but everyone will profit from it. This is the most basic kind of peace work.

I would like to leave you with one last reflection. One afternoon at the beach while enjoying the warm sun and cool breeze, I noticed a group of young children playing near the breaking waves as they splashed the sandy shore. The children were busy playing and shouting with excitement at the top of their voices as each wave came close, then they jumped sideways to avoid it. There were a few brave ones "testing the waters" who would venture forward to touch the oncoming foam then retreat quickly in caution. These same children just a few minutes later were engulfed in the ocean's salty waters and were enticing the others to join them. Most of the other children followed this invitation and also found themselves surrounded in shallow waves of sand and sea. The few remaining children continued jumping sideways to avoid the water's touch.

While I watched these children, I began reflecting back on my own trials at learning to swim. I was captivated by the courage many of these children displayed. I remembered how I always seemed to "step sideways" to avoid confronting my parents and myself. I thought if only I had had the courage to plunge in the water trusting I would be safe, then maybe I would have learned how to *trust myself*. Just at that moment I heard my little child within say, "Barbara! You have been as courageous as any of these children. Every child has special gifts to share. Some children hear the voice of strength and courage; some envision the future; some whisper truths of wisdom; while others touch the stars. OUR gifts are still unfolding...."

Gifts From The Child Within

Children, Children
    What do you see?

    Rainbows and butterflies
    Mushrooms and cherry pies
    Fairies' wings and candy tree

    These are things that children see.

Children, Children
    What do you hear?

Thunder and kitten's purr
Ice Cream bells and silence stir
Flowers bloom and spirits near

These are things that children hear.

Children, Children
    What do you feel?

    Sun rays and Mother's cheek
    Ocean air and excitement's peak
    Shooting stars and joy areal

    These are things that children feel.

Children, Children
    What do you know?

    Laughing faces mean fun
    Love, Joy, and Peace are One
    Only when all truths are told

Will your reality unfold.

Barbara Sinor, 1981

Afterword

The issue of childhood sexual molestation and the therapeutic recovery of its survivors is of foremost interest and concern for therapists and mental health professionals. The statistics for the private and public reporting of incestuous behavior continues to rise as the stigma of acknowledging and breaking the silence of being a survivor is lessened. Because there is a greater understanding by medical and professional caretakers as they become more adept and equipped to deal with the healing and recovery process of the survivor, more survivors are speaking out and sharing their abuse.

Social and personal denial and suppression of such abuse have begun to give way to acknowledgement and validation (Courtois, 1988). With this trend of remembering, reviewing, and recovering from childhood sexual abuse, the therapeutic community is being called to integrate assorted theoretical approaches using a greater number of modalities in pursuit of guiding the incest survivor through the recovery process. Research indicates incest survivors have often not felt heard or understood when seeking assistance from healthcare professionals (Zaleski, 1995). Much more energy has been directed toward understanding the effects of incest then toward evaluating treatment interventions (Fera, 1990).

My recent doctoral research study found transpersonal or psychospiritual forms of counseling and self-help interventions to be advantageous to the healing and recovery from sexual molestation/incest in childhood. These findings have profound ramifications for therapists working with adults who have experienced childhood sexual abuse and other traumatic events in childhood, or even adulthood.

The multidimensional nature of incest, touching symptoms of the social, physical, emotional, mental, and spiritual levels, requires the use of a multifaceted intervention plan. Evidence is growing that one can no longer treat a single dimension without regard to the interaction of each dimension with the other, given the intricacy and complexity of human functioning. Least of all the spiritual dimension

(Westgate, 1996). The therapeutic healing process of survivors of childhood incest benefits by including a holistic approach which addresses all aspects of counseling including the transpersonal or psychospiritual. Literature indicates that a multiple intervention program is preferred and therapists are employing various techniques from several theoretical concepts to assure the survivor's symptoms will be treated and the recovery process initiated.

Often during the therapy process of any orientation, incest survivors experience *spiritual awakening* along with other psychological changes. Even the discussion and reliving of incest memories can bring about a sense of the spiritual for a survivor (Ganje-Fling & McCarthy, 1996). Many times the survivor is not spiritually developed enough to relate feelings in terms of a spiritual phenomenon but may instead talk of a deeper sense of meaning of the victimization. Just as the psychological development of the survivor tends to be arrested around the age of abuse, so does the survivor's spiritual development (Ganje-Fling & McCarthy, 1996).

It must be remembered that whatever the orientation or the methodology used by the therapist to treat the survivor, caution is required surrounding the issues of religion and spirituality. In their article entitled, *Impact of Childhood Sexual Abuse on Client Spiritual Development: Counseling Implications,* Ganje-Fling & McCarthy (1996) summarize:

> Addressing spiritual issues within the counseling process involves accurate, ongoing assessment of spiritual functioning and relevant interventions that are used with discretion and with respect for client beliefs. Consideration must always be given to the counselor's skills and role and to client needs in choosing the degree and type of spiritual interventions employed during counseling. (p. 257)

In my research study of the participants who answered they had utilized psychospiritual counseling methods or self-help techniques during their recovery process, 95% indicated that these interventions were advantageous to their recovery (Sinor, 1997). This exceptionally high percentage implies that the inclusion of psychospiritual treatment modalities when working with survivors is highly beneficial. An eclectic and broad range of methods was noted to be the most successful treatment plan as perceived by the survivors who participated in this study. The findings suggest it would be beneficial for therapists to investigate a holistic approach when working with the survivor population, broadening their scope of treatment to include psychospiritual treatment modalities. The participants of this study clearly felt therapists need to investigate and offer a wide range of intervention techniques, both traditional and psychospiritual, to help facilitate the recovery process.

The research findings also indicate that a majority of the survivors who participated in this research wish to continue and/or begin psychospiritual therapy. Of those who responded to the question of whether they would choose psychospiritual counseling currently, 93% indicated *Yes*. This high percentage indicates a need for more therapists willing to venture into the realm of psycho spiritual counseling. This challenge is for all therapists to consider. The task is not to become a theologian, clergy, or a pastoral counselor. The therapist is being presented with the opportunity of assisting the survivor in integrating her spirituality in such a way as to promote growth and well-being on all levels. This is an admirable task.

It has been established that survivors' psychological recovery may instigate the further development of a spiritual awareness. Abuse survivors often experience spiritual change along with psychological change during the course of therapy; for some, discussion of incest memories is the beginning of a spiritual awakening (Ganje-Fling & McCarthy, 1996). This unveiling of the spiritual can develop at any time before, during, or after professional counseling. Many participants of this sturdy commented on the positive effects that their newfound spiritual nature had on their outlook toward themselves and the world.

Today, there are signs that after a long and tumultuous courtship, spirituality and psychology may be finding common ground. As psychospiritual assessments and techniques become more standard in the treatment of survivors, this population can move forward on the road to recovery. The following quote from one survivor who participated in my study clearly expresses what many others shared:

> Conventional psychology helped me attain tools to *cope* with my experience. But spiritual disciplines and applications provided me with the opportunity to *heal*; not just cope. A spiritual foundation helped me answer my burning questions in a way that leaves me satisfied. Relieving my sense of defectiveness in comparison to others who are not survivors. Freeing me to integrate my experiences into my consciousness, fully utilizing them as a part of my life as positive aspects of my life, from which I could generate much power and beauty.
>
> Psychology in its conventional state felt much life plastic surgery for the soul. Spiritual exploration and discipline taught me nothing is imperfect. And rather than striving for the standard of psychological correctness that psychology taught me I could never quite measure up to, spiritual discipline gave me opportunities to experience a sense of perfection reaching for deeper than social standards. (Sinor, 1997, p. 97)

The research findings from my study introduce a new base of knowledge surrounding the treatment of survivors. First, that psychospiritual interventions can be advantageous to the survivor's recovery process. Second, a multiple treatment approach of these methods is recommended. Lastly, that it would be beneficial for therapists working with the survivor to offer psychospiritual interventions such as found in this book *Gifts From The Child Within* and the follow-up book *An Inspirational Guide for the Recovering Soul*, in addition to traditional modes of counseling. These findings can be used by social and professional health providers to broaden viewpoints and help determine a more holistic treatment plan for the survivor population of childhood sexual abuse.

Further research data is needed in the area of transpersonal/ psychospiritual counseling which may help healthcare professionals understand the motivation, needs, and healing process of those seeking therapy relating to childhood sexual abuse and incest. It is hypothesized that for mental health providers to help their clients who are dealing with negative childhood experiences realize their full recovery potential the exploration of the psychospiritual quality of human existence needs to be included in the therapy process. It is clear that the research findings from my doctoral research study can be used a sa guidepost toward the holistic care and treatment of the incest survivor, as well as, those suffering from other post-traumatic symptoms.

A final thought I would like to present to the reader surrounds the publication of an accompanying book to *Gifts From The Child Within* titled *An Inspirational Guide for the Recovering Soul* (Astara, Inc. 2003). This book is a continuation of healing exercises, suggestions, and rituals presented in an easy "open to any page" format. I appreciate the extraordinary and creative ways survivors of trauma choose to process their present and past emotions which present during therapy. I am encouraged to share some of the techniques these brave women and men employ, as well as, to share many of the healing exercises I have suggested to my patients for inspiration, healing, and recovery. The guidance found within this follow-up book is intended to stimulate *action* toward discovering a path of well-being and spiritual balance. My future books to watch for include *What's Really Going On? Questioning Our View of Addiction* which is a co-authorship with a dear friend, Deborah McCloskey and *Tales of Addiction*. These two books take the reader to the depths of addiction and the highs of recovery through personal stories.

Barbara Sinor, Ph.D.

References

Courtois, C.A. (1988). *Healing the Incest Wound: Adult Survivors in Therapy.* New York: W.W. Norton & Company.

Fera, E. (1990). "Self-Help as an Intervention for the Long-Term Effects of Incest." *Dissertation Abstracts International, Vol. 51-06B,* p. 3128. (University Microfilms No. AAG9022229)

Ganje-Fling M. & McCarthy, P. (1996). "Impact of Childhood Sexual Abuse on Client spiritual Development: Counseling Implications." *Journal of Counseling & Devlopment, Vol. 74,3.* VA: American Counseling Association.

Sinor, B. (1993). *Gifts From The Child Within, 1st Ed..* CA: Moon Dance Publishing.

Sinor, B. (1997). "A Psychospiritual Perspective for the Therapeutic Recovery Process of Adult Female Incest Survivors." *Research Abstracts International, Vol. 23, Issue 3,* p. 858. (University Microfilms No. LD03810)

Sinor, B. (2003). *An Inspirational Guide for the Recovering Soul.* CA: Astara Publishing, Inc.

Westgate, C. (1996). "Spiritual Wellness and Depression." *Journal of Counseling & Development, Vol. 75, 1.* VA: American Counseling Association.

Zaleski, J.L. (1995). "Breaking the Rule of Silence: The Healing Process of Adult Female Survivors of Childhood Incest." *Masters Abstracts International, Vol. 34-04,* p. 1557. (University Microfilms No. AAIMM06175)

About the Author

Dr. Sinor has maintained a private counseling practice for over twenty-five years. She counsels individuals exploring the healing and recovery of Addictions, Post Traumatic Stress Disorder, childhood abuse/incest, adult children of alcoholics, and codependent/self-esteem issues.

Dr. Sinor is coauthor of *Beyond Words: A Lexicon of Metaphysical Thought* and author of the follow-up book, *An Inspirational Guide for the Recovering Soul.* This book is a companion guidebook for further growth and understanding of the personal healing and recovery process which can be used by anyone dealing with past or present trauma. Barbara coauthored the manuscript *What's Really Going On? Questioning Our View of Addiction* and currently is working on her fifth book *Tales of Addiction* which documents personal stories from those who have been or are addicted to drugs and/or alcohol, or those whose life has been affected by addiction through friends and family.

Dr. Sinor received her Doctorate in Psychology at the Southern California University for Professional Studies in 1997. She received her Master of Arts degree in John F. Kennedy University's Graduate School for the Study of Human Consciousness majoring in Transpersonal Counseling Psychology. She graduated with honors from Pitzer College receiving her Bachelor of Arts degree with a double major in Sociology and Women's Studies. Barbara is a Clinical Hypnotherapist certified by The American Council of Hypnotist Examiners and The Hypnotists Examining Council of America.

Barbara encourages your comments and can be contacted by email through her web site at www.DrSinor.com or writing to: P.O. Box 382 Middletown, CA 95467.

Index

N

natural transformation, 36, 39
negative patterns, 190
nightmares, 142, 149

O

over-protectiveness, 164

P

passive-aggressive, 166
Peck, M.S., 79
personal power
    acknowledging, 165
physical abuse, 19, 40, 83, 102
    recovery, 4
Pinocchio, 21
psychospiritual counseling, 220,
    221, 223
psychospiritual integration, 61
psychospirituality, 59–61
Psychosynthesis, 36
psychotherapy, 39, 40, 213, 215
Puddingstone Dam, 3

R

rationalization, 9
reality
    conspiracy, 186
    creating, 185
Re-Creation Therapy™, 20, 33–
    49
    and hypnotherapy, 40
    and reality, 185
    case study, 76
    codependency, 124
    conscious self-transformation,
        62
    development, ix
    dream work, 176
    stages, 186
    transpersonal aspect, 62
ritual, 118, 130, 132, 143, 173
Roberts, J., 55
Rubin, L., 71
rules, unwritten, 47

S

scripting, 96, 98
self-esteem, 73
    and alcoholic parent, 83
    creating, 79
    defined, 77
self-hate, 146, 163
self-hypnosis. *See* autohypnosis
self-image, 71–79, 94, 171
    exercise, 173
    labels, 71
    negative, 208
    re-creating, 20
sexual abuse, 101, 102, 190,
    191, 193, 219, 222, 223
sexual molestation. *See* incest
shame, 146–49
    and abuse, 96
    and forgiveness, 162
    emotional saboteur, 137
    inner child work, 40
should/shouldn't, 74–77
spastic colon, 141
spinal malformation, 149
spiritual abuse
    recovery, 4
stress management exercises,
    139
subconscious memories, 26, 186
subconscious mind
    and reality, 35
    and time-travel, 204
subconscious pattern, 34
substance abuse, 83
Sufi, 126
suppressed sex education abuse,
    101, 102, 106

T

Transactional Analysis, 5
Transpersonal Counseling, x, 225
transpersonal guide, 62–64
transpersonal-self, 60, 65–68,
    189
trauma
    recovery, 4
traumatic past, 42
triggered victimhood, 95–97
true self, 14–16
Twelve Step programs, 80